PRAISE

for

A Conversion From Mind to Soul

What a story, what a journey, what extraordinary revelations! Rev. Judy's book is so POWERFUL and I truly resonate with all that she revealed through her experiences. Rev. Judy has done a masterful job of covering every aspect of the human journey, every emotion, and every challenge we encounter with our earthly existence. Her book is written with care, love, wisdom, sensitivity, openness, and profound insightfulness for the reader.

> —Rev. Zemoria Brandon, LCSW, administrator, and media relations liaison for the Sickle Cell Disease Association of America; co-author of, "Non-Pharmacologic Management of Sickle Cell Pain," published in the *Hematology Journal*, "Blood, 2002 and the *New England Journal of Medicine*, 2003. Rev. Brandon is appointed as the honorable Naa DeDe Ota 1, member of the Asere Royal Family and Queen of Ajenkotoku in Accra,Ghana.

What a skillful narrative. It conjures up images of a giant ferris wheel, as it transports people through the highs and lows of life. Every emotion is felt in that short rotation; just like the book which permeates through every fibre of our being, bringing alive each experience. Rev. Judy's insightful and respectful writing resonates with all readers everywhere as she reflects the Oneness of the Human Family in their hopes and aspirations, highs and lows.

> —Rev. Farida Ali, Interfaith Minister; Principal Representative to the United Nations for the All Pakistan Women's Association(APWA) and member of World Council Religions for Peace

Rev. Judy is one of the great Masters. She writes from the heart and teaches the reader how to live an egoless life free from fear. While sharing her stories and lessons learned, Rev. Judy compassionately holds your hand and guides you down your spiritual path. She lovingly points out the pot holes along the way, leads you to solid ground, and then gently places you in God's pocket for safekeeping. This is a powerful guidebook and a blessing to read!

—Jo Ruddy, Ph.D., Metaphysical teacher and spiritual coach. Founder of Counseling Concepts, LLC, Tucson, AZ

A CONVERSION FROM
MIND
TO
Soul

**Three Steps to
Recognizing and
Bringing Forth Your
Soul's Desire**

REV. JUDY MILLER-DIENST

DEDICATION

With gratitude, I dedicate this book first to my God of many names who always stands with me and works through me.

To my son, Jim, who is my favorite connection to this world. Being your mother is my greatest achievement and honor.

To Kenny and James, my grandsons, who are the magnificent embodiments of Spirit. I am honored to witness your God-selves and grateful we share the same Soul group.

To all the Beings that came before me, to all the Beings here now, and to all the Beings that will follow, I say NAMASTE, which means "the Soul within me recognizes and honors the Soul within you."

In Loving Memory of

Kenneth L. Miller
1949–2009

And

Lillian E. Neil
1925--2012

ACKNOWLEDGMENTS

Bonnie Gold Bell and David Sun Todd, my dear friends, metaphysical authors and artists, amazing creators, and Beings of Light—I thank you for your faith in me, your powerful healings, messages from Spirit, your influence in this book, and your loving friendship. I have enjoyed being in co-creatorship in our Soul connection all ways and always.

My appreciation and love also go to Bonnie Olson, Carol Lord, and Jane Lord—your loving support and our many laughs together have helped me more than you can imagine. My Soul has grown and healed through your presence in my life. (Unfortunately my friend Jane transitioned this past year. *I miss you Jane and I believe you are now dancing with the angels.*)

I thank my dear Soul Sister and friend, the Reverend Zemoria Brandon, for all the philosophical chats we have shared for hours on end—I love our Soul talks. I am so proud of you. You are a continual reminder to me to always say, "*yes.*"

To Jo Ruddy, Ph.D.—thank you for holding the dream with and for me.

To Judy Meyers, R.N., my backup coordinator for the Sacred Distance Healing Circle, and to all members of this healing group—I give heartfelt thanks for your commitment to serve humanity through your dedication to helping all Souls in need.

I am deeply grateful to all the directors and deans at The New Seminary for Interfaith Studies, New York, from 2009 to 2011. Deep, lifelong friendships were developed with my fellow ministers during our seminary journey.

Deep gratitude goes to my editors, Barbara Ardinger, Ph.D. (www.barbaraardinger.com) and Linda Carlson (Carlsonedit@gmail.com) and to my proofreader, Jodi Hardy.

I also thank my family, spiritual community, and past friends and relationships for bringing my Soul the fears and challenges that were the catalysts for this book and the fodder for my growth.

I thank my clients for believing in me and my students for teaching me.

Finally, a big thank you to everyone who supported me in my dream of creating this book. Thanks also to those of you who reviewed and critiqued the manuscript. Your input has been invaluable.

CONTENTS

PREFACE

As we step out of the rambling busyness of the mind (the 10,000 things the Tao refers to) and center ourselves in our hearts, we are able to drift gently to our Soul, where we discover our true self.

A Conversion from Mind to Soul not only gives us the opportunity to respect the mind but also teaches us to receive a deep feeling of adoration for our glorious Universal-Soul. This book shows us how we may move from one to the other with ease and grace.

Let us calm the mind, free the fears, and find the freedom within ourselves to claim our good. We deserve to have a personal awareness, connection, and deep relationship with our Soul—that intimate, powerful, loving connection that is our spiritual center. Please allow yourself to step onto a journey of Soul Discovery.

My intention is to acknowledge the many levels of fear that may affect every human being. For some, sharing their greatest fear is their greatest fear. I will write about some common fears that can dominate your life and suggest ways to move out of them and into love. In *A Conversion from Mind to Soul* we will explore how to:

- Move from Fear to Faith. Fear permeates our world. To live in fear destroys. To live in faith creates, heals, and saves us and all of humanity.
- Discover your Soul's Desire. We all want to know why we are here. What is our Soul? What does it desire?
- Create Connection. Humans desire to reach out to others and to connect. We are all on a search to fully connect to God and to our own Soul.

You always have choice. In the chapters that follow, you will discover many opportunities to be aware of the power of your words and thoughts. You will discover how change is necessary to bring forth the life you desire. What was, was. It is part of your story. Create a new story beginning now.

As an interfaith minister, I honor all paths. God answers to many names. You do not have to believe in any tradition or religion to connect with the Universal Life Force Energy, because It is the very life within you at this very moment. It is the spark of life energy that *is* you. When we are in nature, with animals, with plant life, connecting with the Earth, whether beside the sea or on a mountaintop, it is that which we are breathing in, smelling, touching, seeing, feeling, and connecting to that is the energy we call by all the sacred names. Throughout this book, I may use many sacred names as I reference the Divine One.

I come to you with the experience of many years of living in fear, many years on the path of healing these fears and knowing that as long as I am living in this physical expression as a human being, I will be facing and working through new fears. The gift I bring you is not only what I have learned during my own challenges and continued healing opportunities on mind, body, and spiritual levels, but also the witnessing of my clients over the last twenty-plus years as they, too, have healed deep wounds. They have moved past where they imagined they could heal.

I bring you hope, truth, knowing, and the opportunity to accept your own healing. Your path is your path, and the choices you make determine what your path is. I cannot change your path for you, but if you are determined to change the path you are currently on, I can show you the way.

My own background is eclectic. As far back as I can remember, I felt different because I "knew" things before or while they were happening to others. As an intuitive child, I had a deep understanding of why certain things were happening in my life. No one in my family or circle of friends displayed intuitive abilities. However, that did not stop my curiosity and thirst for learning more about the other realms. So here I am, way down the road, as it were, realizing with great delight and wonderment that I have never been afraid of my intuitive gifts. This, I have learned, is generally not the case for others. I must have healed fear of intuition issues in my many past lifetimes, which enables me to bring forward today the safety and knowing of Truth for others who want to find their intuitive self and their brilliant Souls without fear.

In the mid-1970s, after moving from rural Ohio to busy Southern California, I began meeting people and taking classes that soon led me to an understanding of my intuition. I had a deep remembering. My Soul contract was surfacing. Everything was changing. *I was changing.* For the last forty years, I have been propelled forward faster than I could ever have imagined. In 1999, when I had the life-changing opportunity to look at my fears on a very deep level, I came to the realization that a lot of the emotional and physical dysfunction in my family dynamics had definitely affected my life. I had to face the fears that were entrenched deep in my belief system—in my subconscious—and played out in my life. As I discovered my past life experiences, Soul-group connections, emotional and physical family issues, I had even more awareness that I needed and wanted to change.

Being clairvoyant, clairsentient, and clairaudient, and having prophetic knowing (more information on this later) gives me the opportunity to serve in this world by bringing guidance to others from the God energy. I do this in various intuitive ways. Always providing us with what we need to know, Spirit dictated this book to me for you to read and for us all to follow as we walk our personal growth paths. I receive messages coming for others from the energetic representation of God that calls itself *The Council.*

Spirit led you to this book. There is a message somewhere in here for you from Spirit. May you find what you are seeking in the stories and messages contained within these pages.

"What you are seeking, is seeking you."

—Jalaluddin Rumi[1]

My intention is to bring you into awareness of your Soul. When you release your deepest fears, you unlock the door, move the mountain, and release what no longer serves you. My prayer for you is to discover your true self and to move into alignment with your Source and your Soul.

There may be times when you need to take a few minutes to process the messages in this book. Please allow yourself to do so as needed.

The following message was channeled from *The Council*[2] in 2005:

> *Many humans carry anger and hatred in their hearts. Through that very activity, they project it outward into the collective consciousness of the world. The fear, hatred, and anger fester and grow.*
>
> *There is controversy regarding whether to allow this destructive information into your awareness*

---

1   Jalaluddin Rumi, thirteenth century Sufi poet and mystic. The quote is from *Essential Rumi* by Coleman Barks (Harper One: 1995).

2   The Council is the name of the group of spiritual guides given to the Reverend Judy Miller-Dienst.

and into your presence. This hatred is fed by your unconscious anger and pain. God knows no hatred, anger, or pain. God knows no evil, judgment, or lack. Therefore, if you connect with fear-based mentality, you are not connected to your Source or the absolute Truth of your Soul. You may feel that a part of you is missing.

By turning your back on the media's control of the world's emotions and staying in the Truth of the laws of the Universe, you can contribute something different to your society. We are not suggesting you completely ignore what is happening in your world. Be cautious in your connection to that which destroys. Those that say they want to stay informed are really saying they are comfortable in and with the fears of the world at this time in their life. We are not here to judge them, but to say that possibly by watching the atrocities that are inflicted on others; they can somehow reach the pain within themselves where the atrocities that were inflicted upon them still live.

All paths are different. To allow all others to have their experiences and to allow them to examine their inner pain, via the pain in the world, is to also allow yourself to heal and examine your wounded-ness.

As you become more aware and awakened, you will discover that you can choose to help eliminate the darkness in the world by avoiding the fear-based anchor thoughts that plague your planet. Go to the light within you, to the Truth of love, and radiate that light outward into every heart of every being on your planet, with the intention of allowing others, even for a moment, to be released from their pain and fear, thereby allowing yourself to move out of fear and into the light of love. As you allow peace to live in your heart and thoughts, you will become more peaceful in your life, your relationships, your community, and your world.

I support you in this Truth, and leave you with the knowing that you are all One and therefore One with the One.

INTRODUCTION

"A man is but the product of his thoughts.
What he thinks, he becomes." [3]

—Mahatma Gandhi

Gandhi's words are the Truth. What we think, speak, and believe creates our reality. When we move from our mind's experience into an awareness of our Soul's experience, we are on the journey toward tremendous personal growth. Just as our very thinking creates the law of our life, so do our fears bring forward more challenging events, more fears, and more traumas. We are responsible for our own health, happiness, and prosperity. We cannot blame others for our life.

Listen to yourself. Take responsibility for your thoughts and behavior. Do you have any idea how you act in this world? Are you at all conscious of the level of energy you project into your community, your family, and your work environment? Do you care? Do you want to change your

---

3   http://quotations.about.com/cs/gandhiquotes/a/bls_gandhi.htm

life but not really want to do the work? Who said it was going to be easy? It is not going to be easy, but it will be worth the effort.

We are not meant to be perfect. No one is perfect. But are you happy with your life as it is? Or is there a deeper voice within you that is asking for change and wants to be heard? Is your Soul tugging on your mental sleeve, trying to wake you up? This lifetime is your chance to make positive change. Take the chance. Face your dark side so you can move to the light that is your Soul. What are you afraid of? Think about your fears. Really think about them. Fears are illusions based in lies. Is this the way you want to live? *Really?* If not, take a deep breath and say aloud, "Yes!" Speak to that deeper part of you that is here and ready for change.

The Seven Deadly Sins

The traditional Seven Deadly Sins are Anger, Envy, Greed, Gluttony, Lust, Pride, and Sloth. These are fear-based, excessive behaviors.

In archery, the term "sin" means to "miss the mark." As human BE-ings, we often "miss the mark" as we walk this life's path. Does that make us "bad"? No, it does not.

God does not judge good or bad. God sees what IS. However, we humans do judge each other and ourselves. For how many centuries has the church called us "sinners"? The term "sinner" has had a negative, degrading impact on society. It brings up the image of a poor, downtrodden Soul walking with his head lowered, shuffling along, lost and rejected. What a terrible image this is. Hold your heads up! Walk tall! We all have made mistakes and missed the mark. However, we can always forgive the situation, others and ourselves, and try again.

In this book, we will examine blocks to positive life experiences, issues like fears of abandonment, intimacy, commitment, relationships, financial issues, forgiveness, health issues, and death and dying. We'll also examine God and spirituality.

Two Primary Emotions

There are only two primary emotions in our world: LOVE and FEAR. All variants of emotions fall into these two categories. Feelings of intolerance, hate, criticism, judgment, revenge, jealousy, and resentment—for example—fall under the energy of FEAR. So do the Seven Deadly Sins. When we are in fear, we are missing the mark regarding our connection to our Source. When we are in connection with the Source, we are dwelling in the other main emotion, LOVE.

Compassion, forgiveness, support, kindness, caring, understanding, and gentleness (to name just a few) are emotions that fall under the energy of LOVE.

We always have choice as to which direction we move in. At times, it feels like we have no choice, but the truth is that, on some level, we always do have a choice. Free will is a God-given gift. We have free will—that is, the choice— to stay connected to God's unconditional love or to stay unaware and disconnected from the Truth, which means we are choosing to live in FEAR.

This book will help you discover how your mind's focus on fear can destroy your health, your finances, and your relationships. Then we will learn how love can bring them all back to you.

~ Part 1 ~

Move From Fear
To Faith

MOVING FROM FEAR TO FAITH

Endless Miracles

In the early morning hours of mid-October 2007, I awakened to an awareness of pressure radiating through my chest from my back, up into my jaw, and into my right shoulder. Guidance led me to take an aspirin and get my phone nearby. Then I promptly went into denial that any terrible thing could be happening to me. So very tired, I got back into bed, trying to make myself comfortable. More than a half an hour passed, and so did the pain, so I said to myself, *See? I'm okay.* Within fifteen minutes, however, the pain started again. I don't know what I was waiting for. I guess I thought there would be huge, mind-blowing pain that would undeniably be a heart attack, yet I knew that heart attack symptoms for women are different from those for men. I continued to rest and wait for way too many hours before I finally got out of bed, showered, and dressed for the day. *I don't have time for this ridiculous situation,* I told myself. Many people have told me that I was not alone in my denial when these symptoms appeared.

After procrastinating and filled with dread, I finally called 911. Paramedics and EMTs soon swarmed my home and hooked me up to the EKG equipment. Within a few moments they carted me off to the hospital, where I was admitted. From that time on, everything was pretty much a blur. After many tests, I was told I would have an angiogram the next morning and maybe a procedure to open an artery.

I have no memory of the trip from the first hospital during the late morning hours of the next day to the second hospital that specialized in open-heart surgeries. I do remember awakening in ICU/pre-op and seeing my family standing around me with terror in their eyes. The cardiologist was there to tell me that I was in a crisis situation. My arteries were ninety-five percent blocked! I was told it was a miracle (my first) that I had lived through hours of heart attack symptoms the previous day.

One by one, the surgeon, the anesthesiologist, and the surgical team members came into my room to introduce themselves and explain the systematic open-heart surgery procedure they would perform on me. I was in deep shock and, needless to say, experiencing tremendous fear. I was also heavily medicated. It was all happening too fast. No time for decisions. No choices were given to me (at least none that I remember). The healthcare workers were all matter-of-fact about what needed to happen if I was to stay alive. The team gathered very quickly, it seemed. I do not remember being taken to the operating room. After a seven-hour surgery, I awoke in the ICU. I was on a ventilator. I was also terrified. I could not breathe. I felt phlegm deep in my throat, but there was no air. I was suffocating and thought that surely I would die. When I tried to raise my hand to get the attention of the attending nurse, I was shocked to realize my hands were strapped down. Frantically, I patted my left hand on the bed, but no one could see me struggling. This was the most terrifying moment of my life. I was awake but could not breathe. It seemed like eternity before the respiratory therapist appeared and suctioned my esophagus through the tube. At some point, I noticed the wall clock directly across the room from me. It was, I also noticed, another twenty minutes of agony before they removed the ventilator. As they pulled the tube out of my throat, I began coughing and gasping for air.

Sometime later, my doctor arrived and told me I had received a "cardiac arterial bypass graft x 5." In non-technical language, that meant I had received *five* bypasses. The second miracle showed itself to me when I was told I had absolutely no heart muscle damage and had had very little blood loss during the surgery. Three days later I was released to a rehab center. I later learned that they had no experience with open heart surgery patients or the special care needed to prevent infection.

After two days in the facility I was in an ambulance again, speeding back to the hospital. Thanks to lack of proper care at the rehab center, a blood clot had moved from my right leg into my right lung. Many medical people have told me that it was a miracle that I lived through the experience of three hours of excruciating pain. You see, I was in pain from three until six in the morning. The rehab night staff ignored my screams for help. They simply had no knowledge as to what my symptoms represented or training in how to help me. Usually when a blood clot releases and moves into a lung, there is one pain and the patient dies. My third miracle! Obviously, I was meant to stay on this planet and in this body a little longer.

My life has changed dramatically since those terrifying days. At first, I experienced a new level of fear. As the weeks and months passed and my sternum began knitting itself back together, my nerves began awakening, and the muscles in my chest and breasts were mending, I felt more excruciating, shooting, stabbing pain. For a while, my emotions were unpredictable, which is to be expected when the physical body and heart chakra are violently split open. There were also many months of grieving, sadness, despair, worry, stress, and loss of time and memory. Deep fear took over where trust and peace used to be.

It wasn't until I understood that this event was my Soul's choice to further deepen my personal growth that I reached some clarity. The experiences and lessons gave me the opportunity to either stay in fear and negativity or find my way back to the truth of whom I am. In my recovery, I revisited my Soul's purpose and learned without doubt my connection to God and my commitment to serve.

It is said that time heals all wounds. This may or may not be so, but as we take time to learn to release negative thinking, and move into the light and the energy of God's unconditional love, we may then move into joy, forgiveness, faith, gratitude, and peace. I will always be grateful to my excellent doctors and healthcare providers. I am grateful to my friends and family for spending countless hours with me, both physically and by telephone, as I struggled to find my inner center again. Through countless visits, gifts of food, and energy healings, they brought me humor, love, strength, prayer, and support when I needed it most. My clients and students also supported me through their healings and love. I am so thankful.

I have fully recovered from those days when my physical and mental bodies were completely jeopardized. However, I know without a doubt that my Spirit within always remained intact. Experiencing a heart attack, open-heart surgery, and a blood clot to the lung, yes, I was afraid I was going to die. I then remembered that *we never die*. Our Spirit lives on eternally.

Create a Healing Journal

I encourage you to create a healing journal to use during your experience with this book. Document your thoughts and the feelings that surface as you learn techniques and receive ideas. Certain statements may trigger you.

Document what and how you feel. Every day, make a list of what you are grateful for. Stay present in your life. Stay in this moment.

Here is your first opportunity for a journal entry. Take a moment to make a list of your top ten (or more) fears. Then think about and list what you would be afraid of anyone else finding out about you. Under each item, list what it is that you think created that fear and that circumstance. In truth, the fears you do not want to face, those that make you feel the most uncomfortable and vulnerable, are exactly issues you need to address. Making your list (becoming aware) is your first step toward releasing your fears.

What Is Fear?

Fear leads us to the dark side. Fear holds us back. Fear holds us down, tortures us, chews us up, spits us out, buries us, and dances on our graves. It keeps us from our Divine Potential. *Where there is fear, there is no freedom.* Where there is fear, there are ignorance, intolerance, anger, and hatred. Fear creates unnecessary pain and destructive behavior toward oneself and others. Fear may be your experience, but it does not have to be your Truth.

Initially, we learned fear as a way to protect ourselves from pain. The example of touching a hot stove makes this point. We got burned. Then intelligence kicked in, and we knew not to touch the hot stove again, because in the past doing so brought pain. However, we continue to metaphorically "touch the hot stove" each time we continue to choose the same destructive and sabotaging behavior from our past. Please allow me to paraphrase a quote attributed to Albert Einstein, *Insanity is when we continue to perform the same behavior, expecting a different outcome.* If we continue to live in the pain of our childhood and still listen to old stories of what was, we will be fearful of what we may find in the present moment. The power is in the ability to remain present. It is always your choice to stay here, in the moment, in this now, or to move backward in time, into the past, or drift into the fantasy of the future. There is no reality in either the past or the future. The only reality is here and now, where God resides.

Do you fear not being good enough, smart enough, pretty enough, or successful enough? When we carry these fears, shame and guilt can push their way in. Where there is shame, there is self-loathing. Shame comes from the outside and says something is wrong with me. When we carry shame, we cannot function or move forward. Shame carries one of the lowest vibrations on our planet.

Guilt says there is something wrong with what I have done. If we have done something that is contrary to love energy—guilt usefully teaches us that we need to change, make amends, and release the negative behavior. Those who try to make us feel guilty, however, carry fear themselves and would prefer to have us stay limited and never experience our Divine True Self. When we live our lives coming from love, kindness, and the light, with harm to no one, there is never a reason to feel guilt.

When we fear lack, we lack faith. We doubt that God

will supply us with everything we need. Fear of death is doubt that there is eternal life. The fear of loss of anyone and anything is attachment to the belief that there is not enough.

Many fears surfaced while I was writing this book. I feared criticism. Then I remembered that only human egos criticize. God never criticizes. God always supports us in our choices. The Universe always says, "YES." I also remembered I must stop being fearful of disappointing others, be true to myself, and continue to write and speak Source's words.

Fear of being wrong, of being criticized, judged, punished, of looking foolish, making a mistake, being unloved, unappreciated, of being poor, homeless, and alone are definitely parts of the human condition— the collective consciousness of this planet. I have feared all of these things and more. However, I refuse to claim them as my reality any longer.

Awareness is the first step toward healing.

The Dark Side of Ego

In my references to ego, I am not referring to the ego self that demonstrates the very light within each of us, the Soul's true personality and the Divine essence of who we are. I am not referring to our personality, which is that part of us that expresses from a loving center.

When we say that a person has a negative personality, we are witnessing that person's fear acted outward through their negative ego self. There are many types of ego. Most serve us very well. However, in this book, when I speak of the ego, I am referring to a side of ego that is not pleasant. This is the ego that carries the fear, doubt, disbelief, and distrust. I say it comes from the Dark Side. This ego can be identified as the one that dances with delight when you are in emotional, physical, or spiritual pain. As Marianne Williamson writes, "The ego is merely a fearful thought."[4]

I would like to be clear that I do not believe in "killing" the ego. (That concept is destructive and ego-based.) Ego is never defeated. It simply is. What we need to do, however, is move the negative ego self into a different compartment of our mind. We will always have a glimmer of ego as human beings. However, instead of a monster-sized ego, let's change it into a pea-sized ego.

"Lower self" is another term for ego. It is that part of us demonstrated by endless thinking. It can keep us awake at night with its continuous mind chatter. This mind activity pulls us right out of the present moment and sends us backward into the past or pushes us forward into an unknown future where worry may be lurking. Ego does not want us to notice its behavior, and after a lifetime of on-going inner chatter, most people no longer are aware of it. We can become ensconced in egoic thought. The thoughts you think you think are the ego. The ego knows that if we become fully aware of it, it will indeed be diminished and

---

4   Marianne Williamson, *A Return to Love, Reflections on the Principles of A Course in Miracles*, Ch. 3 (New York: 1992, HarperCollins, 1992).

eliminated from its current power position, and it knows that through our awareness, it can become frozen in the snow of our self-discipline. It is ego's desire to keep us disconnected from our true self.

The ego says, *I am what I have. I cannot live without my stuff. I am my job. I am what I look like. I am what others think of me. I am what I drive. I am my bank account. I am my address. I am my body.*

But life is not dependent upon a body, except for this physical experience. Ego identifies with the body through vanity. Attachment to materialism is not God-consciousness; it is ego-consciousness. Ego keeps us dissatisfied and always needing and wanting more. We feel we cannot be filled up. We feel empty. We feel lesser-than. I believe countless numbers of people are addicted to the ego. (Jesus was the exception.) However, ego will not allow you to admit to your addiction because if you admit it, you may have to change. This level of ego does not want you to change.

Only humans have ego. Everything else just *is.* Everything else exists in the flow without doubt. Animals love unconditionally. They grow, cycle into death and rebirth, without questioning how, why, or when. As awareness of the Divine grows within us, the ego diminishes. Trust this Truth and stay aware of your thoughts.

To assist us in changing the negative collective story, we all have an opportunity to stand in the Truth, in the awareness of necessary change in our own life, our thinking, our behavior, and our consciousness as we serve each other and our planet.

Denial Ain't Just a River in Egypt[5]

Denying that a greater consciousness exists will keep you in the illusion of lack, materialism, fear, seeking, wanting, depression, pain, mental suffering, loneliness, and unhappiness. Knowing that a greater Divine Intelligence created everything and wants nothing but happiness, abundance, and health to exist fully in your life will give you a sense of peace, safety, and well-being. Do you deny that God will take care of all challenges in your life? Most likely, you have done so at some point. Humans want it their way and on their time schedule. We think we know what is best. How silly we are! Just imagine for a moment how it would feel to know for certain that an energy greater than yours, a mind more intelligent than yours, a power stronger than you, actually knows what's best for you, yet allows you to make your own choices. Now imagine that one of the choices you make is to move out of denial and into alignment with this greater power. As you do so, you then move into trust and surrender. You learn to receive and believe guidance. And you learn to live in peace. How would that feel?

SHERRY

When Sherry first came to me for counseling, she shared that the critical ego had filled her mind with negativity throughout her entire life. She claimed that her family

---

5   This quote is often attributed to Mark Twain.

13

dynamics were so dysfunctional that they were played out in alcoholism, depression, violence, suicide, and anxiety in one form or another with every family member. Her ego did not want to release this negative thinking. It held on for dear life, justifying its behavior and denying the Truth of who she really is—a divine expression of Source. After each session, when we had cleared negative beliefs and healed emotional wounds, Sherry would have physical manifestations of pain and discomfort, along with manifestations of more and varied negative thoughts. Ego was fighting for its life, its existence. This dark, negative energy of the ego mind-stuff weakens us and makes us feel useless, undeserving, and miserable.

This reminds me of the analogy of a bucket full of crabs. Every time a crab attempts to crawl up out of the bucket, other crabs pull him back down. He just can't get out. Have you ever had this happen to you? Just when you start to change your negative thoughts to positive, ego flares up and you hear a terrible fear-based voice in your head that pulls you right back down into the deep, dark bucket of worry, despair, and depression.

In time, and with patience on Sherry's part, along with a strong commitment to be the winner in this struggle against the ego's negativity, she experienced a big shift and a very different, joy-filled life. All of her relationships changed for the better. She experienced a greater sense of spiritual connection. Her levels of prosperity and abundance in all things escalated. Sherry learned how to keep the inner critic quiet. She learned how to stay in the present.

Self-Talk

You create your own reality all the time. When your negative inner thoughts, your inner critic, ego, mind-stuff, monkey-mind, the accuser, the enemy, the dark-side, or the devil—call it what you will—is present in your life, life will appear to be challenging.

Every moment, we manifest what we think, feel, and speak. The Universe always says, "*YES!*" We always have choice as to what we allow into our thoughts and what we create in our lives. You may think you don't have any choices or that it's impossible to stop the negative thinking. You are mistaken. God gave us one of the most valuable gifts possible. We were given *free will*. We all have free will—that is, choice—every moment. We can choose to be connected to the Divine Source of All or choose not to connect and stay in the fear and the challenges.

If your self-talk messages go like this—*I am no good, I will never amount to anything, I am a mess. Who would want me?*—please know it is NOT okay to accept this verbal abuse from anyone, including your own inner voice. Stop the self-talk that knocks you down, criticizes you, and judges you. Become your own champion. Fight for yourself! This ego mind has to be controlled. If you don't control it, it will control you. God does not judge you or belittle you. If you judge or belittle yourself or allow others to do this to you, it is time to wake up, step up, and take action for change.

You may feel beaten down because of what happened

to you in the past. You may blame yourself or feel guilty for choices you made in the past. The Source does not judge you. God does not remember your past mistakes. It is time you let go of these thoughts and *stop condemning yourself.* It is time to forgive yourself and make every effort to stop your negative thinking. Make room for Spirit to come into your heart, into your thoughts, and into your life. Replace the negative thinking and self-talk with the words and thoughts of loving-kindness.

We cannot give to others what we do not have. Self-love, forgiveness, and kindness begin within. Too often, religion tells us to love our neighbor, give to others, and be kind to others. Rarely, if ever, are we told to love ourselves and to be kind and giving to ourselves. Instead, we are taught that to love oneself is ego-based and selfish. But it's never too late to learn how to be kind and loving to yourself. Begin with eliminating your negative inner thoughts and quieting the negative inner voice.

Surviving the Shift

I envy the newborns and the children at this time on the earth. I believe this group of Souls is coming into this lifetime knowing who they are and remembering their Divine Connection. The Souls arriving in the last couple of decades are arriving in the midst of the spiritual and planetary energetic shift and are here to help those of us who have been here a lot longer to adjust and cope. They are bringing the wisdom of the ages.

Witness the levels of fear that are currently radiating around the world. Something is coming, and those who do not understand that this change is for the good believe the world is coming to an end. I believe the world is moving into something different from anything we've experienced in our lifetimes and in our parents' and grandparents' lifetimes, too. We are moving into a new consciousness. We are moving into the realization that all that counts is love. The Souls that are consciously on a path of change are, like snakes shedding their skins, releasing old concepts and old beliefs as they are traversing new ground. This shedding must be done as we prepare for the new season on earth. The earth is changing, and we must change with it. This is not comfortable, but it is necessary.

Great numbers of Souls have been departing from this earth as we prepare for the shift. These departures are happening through major cataclysms, environmental disasters, major tragic and fatal accidents, wars, and other attacks on our planet's population. We Souls are always in choice, not only to be on earth at this time, but whether or not to stay here. When our Soul knows it has accomplished its mission here, it goes home. I believe many Souls have chosen to leave with the others in order to assist the Souls that are fearful in their transition.

In any case, it is a time of great upheaval, and we all feel it. Many of us are losing a sense of time. Over the last two or three decades, time seems to have been continually speeding up. I personally have noticed time skipping ahead by months at a time. On January 16 of this year, I called my brother Gary and sang "Happy Birthday" to him on his voicemail. When I answered his return call, Gary sang, "Happy Birthday to Me." I laughed and said, "Yes, bro, Happy Birthday!" He replied, "Thanks, Sis. I'm excited to say that I get to have two birthdays this year." "Really?" I asked. "What do you mean?" I truly did not know what he was talking about. "Well," he said with a laugh, "one today, and the other one on my real birthday, March 16." I had written his birthday down on my calendar two months before it was due. I believe this happened because my brain has been living in a different dimension: *kairos* time (Divine time, i.e., God's time). Many of my clients and students have shared similar experiences.

What do we do during this evolutionary time? We have choices. We can bury our heads deeper in whatever addiction or self-medication we choose to use, or we can choose to move into discovery. We can learn, grow, and move toward the enlightenment that our Soul craves.

Take a moment now to make a journal entry regarding all the marvelous and challenging things you are experiencing at this time of major change. Do you perceive an energy shift? How? List everything, including your questions.

Pay attention.

The First Step Toward Healing

Awareness and knowledge, and the desire to use them make up the first step on the journey to healing.

Here is a powerful tool that is very effective in stopping the egoic mind. Just as when the traffic light turns red, it grabs our attention and halts us immediately—so will the following mental image and your command, halt the inner chatter. Here is how.

Take a deep breath, close your eyes, and envision a traffic light that has turned red, a big, bold, bright red that means STOP. (If you have a challenge with mental imagining, allow yourself to experience the red STOP light through a sound, a feeling, or a knowing.) Each and every time you hear a negative thought, criticism, judgment, blaming, shaming, manipulating, or procrastinating, call the red STOP light into your mind and mentally yell, *STOP!* Or do as I sometimes do. I yell, *"SHUT UP!"* aloud and as loudly as I can.

The negative ego will immediately become quiet. It is as though the ego is saying, *You talkin' to me?* It is surprised you are paying attention. There will be silence. Heavenly silence. If the negative thought returns, repeat the technique. You cannot stop-light yourself to death. The key is to *use the technique*. Just as we need a light switch to turn on the light, we need to use the STOP light technique, along with our voice, to stop the ego.

You cannot change your history, but you can change your relationship with your history. Visualize something else. Rescue yourself from your memories of your past. Dwelling in what no longer exists is the work of the "dark side." It's a total waste of time and energy. It's impossible to be in the present moment when your attention is pulled into what was. *What was is only your story.* The past and the future are illusions. They do not exist. The past is a previous now, and the future is a now that hasn't happened yet. *You only have this moment.* Breathe into this moment. Whatever the appearances are, know that this moment is filled with the energy and love of the Source of All That Is. In this moment, claim that you are safe, you are loved, you are fulfilled, you are richly abundant, and you are whole, healthy, and happy.

Our mind plays many games. Pay attention. Stop the ego. When we learn to stay in the present, we discover there is nothing to fear.

As you become the champion of yourself, you will become conscious of your mind chatter. What is it saying to you? If it doesn't feel good, doesn't sound loving and kind, and doesn't support you in remaining in the present moment, know it is not God energy. Use your red stop light and fill the silence with a loving, kind, self-affirming thought. Then feel the peace.

Fear creates suffering. I paraphrase here when I share that the Buddha taught that pain is inevitable, but suffering is a choice. I interpret this to mean that our physical bodies are temporary, fragile, and vulnerable to harm, injury, decay, and physical pain. Physical pain, loss, and all forms of fear lead to emotional pain. We always have choice in how we perceive our circumstances. We can have control over our emotions, if we choose to.

Oh, the Drama!

Do you create drama, chaos, stress, and intensity in your life? Do you know that you may be addicted to this behavior? When passion and purpose are missing in your life, you may be not only attracted to drama, but also addicted to it. If you are not disciplined in your thought life, you will never have the life you want.

Drama is another way the ego demonstrates itself. You can attract stress, chaos, intensity, and drama/trauma like a magnet attracts straight pins. Do you want drama, or do you want to have a happy life? Use your red stop light. Stop the negative words, thoughts, and feelings and say *NO* to drama, stress, chaos, and intensity now. No one else can do your inner work for you. You can be guided, learn techniques by the hundreds, take endless growth classes, and ask the same questions over and over, but if you don't take action on your own behalf, who will?

When I am asked, "How long will this [growth work] take?" I reassure my questioner by saying what we know deep inside. *We're all on a different, lifelong journey of self-discovery, recovery, and forward movement into Soul and spiritual wholeness. The journey is different for everyone.* Our Soul has chosen this journey for the purpose of continued movement toward enlightenment. The Buddha taught that we could achieve enlightenment in this lifetime. This is good news. Let's do it!

ANGIE

Angie had so much drama in her childhood that she didn't know how to live without it. Her mother and father were alcoholics. There were no boundaries in the home. Angie's older brother would sneak into her door-less bedroom at night to molest her. Angie's younger sister attempted suicide three times by the age of fifteen.

Angie married her first husband, Chuck, another alcoholic, when she was seventeen because she so desperately wanted out of her situation at home. She was three months pregnant with Chuck's child when they married. She believed that if she just loved this man enough, gave him a baby, and was a "good little girl," he would love her, stay with her, and they would live happily ever after.

It was not long before Chuck became physically and emotionally abusive. The beatings caused a miscarriage in Angie's fourth month of pregnancy. The drama continued. Her emotional pain was great. Her fear was huge. However, Angie was luckier than many other young women in the same situation. She got out before she got pregnant again or worse, was beaten to death.

During the next five years of her life, Angie suffered a few months of homelessness and her own addiction to alcohol. She married again, this time to a drug user named Paul. Again, she became pregnant. Again, there were beatings. This time, however, she gave birth to a healthy, beautiful, baby boy. When Paul began threatening the child, Angie knew she had to leave. She took her son and ran.

The drama did not stop there. There were many years of drama and intense fear as she hid from Paul, from her childhood, and from herself while still using alcohol.

Angie is now working hard to change those old mental messages haunting her. She is in recovery. She recognizes the fact that her addiction to substances and to drama have to end. She is practicing what she is learning, and as she lets go of the past and focuses on the moment, where truth is, she finds it easier to breathe. She is finding her center, her peace, and her hope. She is creating a new story for herself and for her son.

Remember to stay in this moment. Live as though this is the only moment you have... *because it is.*

Stress

Stress is a killer. It blocks the flow of good health and well-being. It serves no good purpose. Stress is human-made and ego-based, not God-made. God does not create stress in our lives, nor does God know anything about stress. When we feel stressed we get to look at our choices. No one else can "stress us out"; traffic on the freeways cannot "stress us out"; awful situations cannot "stress us out." Stress is the reaction in our body triggered by our perception of circumstances. We choose to become stressed. Remember that no one else can ever *make* us feel anything that we are not ready to feel.

What buttons are being pushed that take you to stress, anxiety, chaos, or drama? When you feel as though someone or something has triggered a stress-response within you, take a deep breath, then fully exhale, releasing the negative energy from your body. Next, close your eyes and bring the bold red stop light into your mind's eye and mentally shout, STOP. Keeping ego away always reduces the stress experience.

This would be a perfect time to write in your journal about your experiences with stress and the affect it has had on your body, mind, and Soul.

Take a moment now to enjoy the following guided meditation. I suggest that you record yourself reading the meditations offered throughout this book. Playing the recordings back to yourself, instead of reading them, will make it easier for you to be present in the experience. The guided journeys are intended to reduce and eliminate your symptoms of stress and to facilitate the upcoming release processes, and forgiveness exercises.

Guided Meditation #1

Take a deep breath, close your eyes, and relax into the arms of the Divine One. You are supported and loved. Feel Source's presence. Become aware of the beautiful golden light of the Universe moving down into your crown chakra, at the top of your head, then down through your body. This light fills your body, into every cell, moving through and around every organ. Exhale completely.

Slowly take another deep breath and breathe in God's love, and slowly exhale any fear you're feeling.

Slowly take another deep breath. Breathe peace into your heart center. Slowly exhale stress and chaos.

Slowly take another deep breath. Breathe health into your body. Slowly exhale illness.

Slowly take another deep breath. Breathe abundance into your consciousness. Slowly exhale lack.

Slowly take another deep breath. Breathe success into your core. Slowly exhale defeat.

Slowly take another deep breath. Breathe happiness into your heart. Slowly exhale sadness.

Feel the relaxation and the goodness of God moving through you and around you.

Continue to breathe and relax into this very moment. As you focus your attention on your breath, allow silence to surround you. Stay in this space for as long as you are able.

This short, yet effective, breathing meditation is a great little "pocket" tool to remember and use any time life feels overwhelming.

If drama, intensity, guilt, blame, shame, and fear have not worked for you, maybe it is time to try something new. As you change your thinking, you change your experiences. Releasing negative energy from your life allows you to receive awareness of what your Soul wants to create.

Now is the time to get out the list of your ten (or more) greatest fears and how you think they were created. Now follow along on this journey of healing.

Affirmation Prayer

In this moment, I am aware of the Divine Energy of Love. I allow it to surround me and move through me. As I focus my attention on the now and breathe in that which heals me, loves me, and holds me in its Light, I am so blessed.

I allow myself to feel the deep Truth of me...of my Soul. As I discover my Soul, I feel the Light of the Universe not only touching me, but also radiating through me. My Soul vibrates with Love. I feel deep gratitude.

So I say Amen, Ashe, Shanti, Shanti, Shanti.

WHO ABANDONS WHOM?

(BS Affects Your Health)

If you entertain your fears, they will control you. They will affect everything in your life. It is believed that our chakras (energy centers) and our physical body demonstrate the condition of our thoughts and Belief Systems (BS). Our body is a small container around a glorious and powerful energy called Spirit, and Spirit speaks to us continually.

Abandonment is our first emotional wound. From the time our umbilical cord is cut, we experience abandonment. In the womb, we feel at one with our mother. We feel what she feels and assume it is our own feeling. If she is experiencing anger, fear, anxiety, and even abandonment, we will certainly have feelings of anger, fear, anxiety, and an early precursor to the "cutting of the [umbilical] cord" abandonment.[6]

---

6   Dawson Church, Ph.D., *Communing with the Spirit of Your Unborn Child,* 1st ed. (Fairfield, CT: Aslan Publishing, 1988), p. 11.

If our parents, grandparents, great-grandparents—going back seven generations or more—carry a fear, an emotion, or a negative belief system, it will definitely be passed down to us. So it makes sense that as we all go through the physical detachment from our mother at birth, we all therefore suffer abandonment issues to some degree. I have never met a person who does not have some level of abandonment issue.

Let us look at how, through our fears, we experience and express abandonment in our lives and relationships. Our fear of abandonment can create a subconscious attraction to those people that are capable of the act of abandonment.

PAULINE

Over the course of her son Bobby's short life, Pauline had abandoned him at least four times by physically and emotionally leaving him alone with others for years at a time. It is not surprising, therefore, that one of the issues Pauline came to receive healing on was her fear of abandonment when her son committed suicide at the age of nineteen.

Childhood Abandonment

Most of us have seen an infant or small child who notices mommy leaving the room and cries out in pain at the perceived loss of love and connection. We call this separation anxiety. It's perceived abandonment. Everyone experiences this as a small child, whether we remember it or not, and we carry these fears with us throughout our lives. Unfortunate tragedies, such as an early loss of a parent, can be devastating and affect all future relationships.

KATHLEEN

Kathleen's mother died when she was eight years old, and the pain was so great that she blocked the memories of the first eight years of her life. Although she was able to recapture some of her mother's essence through the memories her two younger brothers shared, that did not fill the void. When Kathleen entered into adult relationships, she still carried a great fear of intimacy and fear of abandonment.

Kathleen withdrew, created distance through criticism and blame, then emotionally abandoned her partners. Soon after one relationship ended, she moved into another one, always trying to fill the emptiness and ease her fear of abandonment. Kathleen continually acted out and manifested her greatest fears.

The truth is that we all experience one form of abandonment or another at some point in our lives. Life may bring major loss through death, divorce, or a move across the country when we leave loved ones behind. One person in a relationship may choose not to grow emotionally or spiritually, while their partner chooses to take the forward path. Loved ones may not understand when we set healthy boundaries. All these examples may be perceived as a form of abandonment. Ego will trigger these fears by attempting to keep us in the pain of past abandonment and telling us that abandonment is coming again.

Relationship Abandonment

I was married for twelve years to a man who was very intelligent and nice, but also controlling and passive-aggressive. One of the main reasons our marriage dissolved was because I grew. I was no longer the naïve, immature, twenty-one-year-old he'd married. I took a huge risk and changed. No matter how much my husband wanted me to stay the same, I grew. He feared my changes because he knew on some level that my changing meant he would have to change, too. As I changed, my husband felt abandoned. The relationship could not survive.

Many people fear growing and changing while in a relationship. We fear our spouse will abandon and reject us. We fear he or she may die before we do. We fear being alone. Our negative thoughts take us deep into worry and despair. But when we make a conscious choice to change, we're taking a brave step into the unknown, and this step leads to personal growth. When you hold your hand out for spiritual support, you will receive Divine help. That does not mean you will not have an opportunity to be challenged. It's how we perceive our challenge that determines how rocky the path feels. Let us remember God's promise to straighten all crooked paths.

When we have a strong spiritual foundation, we know

we are never really alone. A healthy relationship has plenty of room for each person to grow, change, and speak their truth. In a healthy relationship, not only will we have the support of our Source, but we will also have the support of our spouse.

We attract and choose relationships according to the wounded or healed emotional level we are currently experiencing. That's a scary thought, isn't it? If we don't take responsibility for what we bring to the table, how can we expect to have healthy relationships? The fear of abandonment can be so overwhelming that we abandon others to save ourselves.

ANNA BANANA

Many years ago, I had a dear friend named Anna who was emotionally fragile. I viewed her as a loving and delightful, childlike Soul. As adults, our "inner children"[7] played well together. We never once had a disagreement of any kind. We called ourselves "kindred spirits."

When Anna entered a new relationship, however, I saw signs of her losing herself. She styled her hair just like her partner's, dressed exactly like her partner, and soon disappeared. Over many months, I called and left numerous messages for Anna. I sent notes asking her to please contact

---

7   I teach the philosophy that our emotions represent the various aspects of ourselves, including our inner children. The tools taught aid with the healing of our emotional woundedness. See www.themysteryschool.org, *5 Step Journey to Healing the Wounded Warrior*, taught through The Mystery School, Inc.

me, to please not leave me. I told her that I would always support her in her choices and in her relationships, but that I did not want to lose her friendship. Anna never answered my calls. I felt very abandoned.

However, as I have ultimately forgiven her and myself and released my pain; I know she had to experience her choices, and her choices were to experience something else. Anna has always been in my heart. I pray she found the Truth of who she really is, under the image someone else asked her to take on and that she accepted in order not to feel abandoned.

I understand that Anna's experience and my experience were individual Soul journey experiences for our own personal growth. As we learn to forgive and let go of the perceived pain and hurt, we heal and learn.

It is said that young Souls get angry with others, old Souls get angry with themselves, but really wise Souls have already forgiven and have moved on.

BOB AND CONNIE

After Bob and Connie had been dating for a couple of months, Bob decided he really didn't want to have a serious relationship with Connie. He shared with her that he found her to be possessive, controlling, and needy. He was willing to be a friend, but that's all. Connie could not accept the idea that they would not be lovers, marry, and grow old together. Even though he had clearly told her they were finished, she hung on to a fantasy that some day he would tell her he loved her. She believed their relationship was getting stronger. Connie followed Bob, repeatedly called him, and spied on him. She spent endless hours fantasizing that he still wanted her and that they were still in a relationship.

Connie's childhood had been filled with abandonment. Her biological father had left when she was one year old, and her young mother had really not known how to raise a child alone. Life for Connie was lonely and scary. She had grandparents and extended family members who tried to pitch in and spend time with her, but they really could not fill the role of the parents. These people, too, would come and go.

Throughout Connie's teenage and young adult years, she developed a very strong, self-defeating pattern. She partied a lot and attracted and fell in love with unavailable men who would leave her feeling abandoned and unlovable. She began some stalking behaviors that frightened even her. Her search for love and consistency in a relationship became her great torment. The demise of her relationship with Bob affected her more than her other break-ups had. As Connie became extremely depressed and anxious she showed strong signs of an obsessive-compulsive disorder. She began using alcohol and drugs to numb the pain. She still refused to release her fantasy of having a relationship with Bob.

Her life has been challenging and filled with many bad choices, but Connie is now beginning to see the major theme of her life. She has also felt disconnected from her spiritual and creative aspects. She has been looking for love outside herself, rather than within. After she hit her low point and reached out for help, she began to awaken to her destructive choices. She began making every effort to reconnect to her true self. She moved into forgiveness. Connie made a choice to change. Change is not easy, and she still has many choices to make as she begins a journey down a new road. But now she is realizing that Source is there to guide and support her and that all things are possible.

Egoless Love

Ego-based love says we are attracted to another person because they have what we want in our own life.

Egoless love means fully accepting the person the way they are without judgment, need, expectation, control, or the desire to change them.

Many years ago, my ego chose a relationship with a person who was in a leadership role. Looking back, I see I was in love with their position, title, and place in the community, as seen by others. But I wasn't in love with the person. When their outer mask slipped, I discovered that I did not really like the person under the illusion. I learned an important lesson.

Have you ever fallen in love with someone because you needed to fill an empty space within yourself? Think about this and journal what you learn.

When we totally accept another person just as they are and not want to change them, we become a better partner. As we look at what it is within our self that needs changing, we become a better person.

Family Abandonment

The torment of betrayal and abandonment by family members can be devastating. We want to trust those people who gave birth to us, raised us, and are part of our Soul group. However, we may discover they are not trustworthy. Our sense of self may be challenged when we see that those who we believe should love us unconditionally either do not know how to love or choose not to love.

Several times in my life I have had family members reject, betray, and abandon me. I have experienced deep emotional and physical pain. As I look back upon my perceived experiences, I question myself regarding my part in the drama. Many times, I simply didn't understand what created their actions. Today, I have the opportunity to grieve, feel my pain, release all negative energy I'm holding onto, and forgive myself and others. I have to remember that humans may leave us, but God never does. Therefore, I chose to reconnect to my Source for support and acceptance of *who I am*.

When I talked about my frustrations regarding my family with my dear friend, David, he—in his deep wisdom—said to me, "Think how much these challenging people must love you to bring you such great opportunities of spiritual growth."[8] What a powerful statement that

---

8   David Sun Todd, transformational artist, author, and metaphysical

was. All I had to say was, "Wow, they must really love me a lot!"

Challenges give us opportunities to remember that the people who are primary characters in our life story are simply Souls on their own growth paths. As we look down the path we have been walking, we may see that some are behind us and some may be ahead of us, but we are all where we are meant to be in this moment. Our challenges, disappointments, and losses give us opportunities to forgive ourselves for being a part of the drama. Remember, the issues are rarely, if ever, about the other person. *Always look within.*

Spiritual Abandonment

Although our perception of spiritual abandonment is painful, we need to remember that spiritual abandonment is an illusion. During challenging times of loss, it's easy to blame God. When things don't go the way we want them to, we blame God. Many hold the belief that God creates our diseases and punishes us. When people have been taught that God is angry, punishing, and mean, how can they feel loved and connected to It?

The energy of the Universe, also known as God, is impersonal. It does not choose favorites. It does not judge and punish. It is not angry. It is simply energy that mirrors back to you what you believe. It agrees with you. It does not fight you. If your focus is on negative thinking, you

healer. See www.bellandtodd.com

will experience more of it. When you calm down, listen, breathe, and relax, you will experience more peace. Life is constantly changing. It's all about your choice of how and what you perceive.

Our Source never leaves us. We leave It. God is eternally present for us. We simply need to realign ourselves with the Universal energy and remember the Truth of our connectedness to the One. Spirit moves through us and as us. Therefore, we are one with the One. When we chose to perceive things differently and remember to integrate this knowing, our fear of spiritual abandonment will subside.

Fear of Being Alone

Fear of being alone is a cousin to the fear of abandonment. An extreme fear of being alone may be demonstrated when a person is suffering physical, verbal, or emotional abuse and yet stays in the relationship. We see this played out in movies, books, in the news, and maybe in our own homes.

It doesn't matter whether it is a woman or a man who is in an abusive relationship. It's always difficult to leave. What makes us stay? There may be many complicated reasons. Some people would rather suffer the terror, humiliation, and nightmare of the abuse than experience being alone. When there is a constant fear of abandonment, we may be willing to sell or prostitute ourselves in our home, job, or relationship.

What does that mean, selling and/or prostituting ourselves?

Will you do anything to keep your spouse, partner, job, or friendship? Do you give your power away? Do you sell yourself short? Will you accept being treated badly in order to not be alone? Do you fear saying *no*? Do you fear speaking your truth? Have you stopped learning and growing? Did you give up on yourself? Are you codependent? Are you boundaryless? Would you rather have *anyone* around rather than be alone? When you fear being alone, you are not aware of the Source's presence. You have lost contact with God and your God-self. Again, remember that God does not leave us, we leave God.

Please take a moment to reflect on all the questions in the previous paragraph. Write all of your answers and awareness's in your journal. Process all your feelings around this issue.

JOHN

A newborn baby is still aware of its God-connection. However, depending upon the treatment and consciousness of the baby's primary caretakers, that baby may not be supported in maintaining its connection. Always searching for connection, we can spend our lives looking outside of self (rather than within) to find someone or something to fill us up. The Soul is seeking to reconnect to its God-self.

As an only child, John was often lonely. His mother and father were too busy with life, their jobs, and their own limitations to being emotionally present. As John grew older and made friends, he was attracted to his best friend's large family. He spent most of his free time at their home. There were many children in the family, and relatives often visited, too. To John, all the activity, noise, and laughter meant more love, more fun, and more protection from being alone.

When John was about thirty, he married a woman from a large family and embraced the companionship of the whole clan. Sadly, he and his wife divorced after ten years. Because John disliked living alone, he was drawn into relationships that led to moving in together rather quickly. His fear of living alone led to making bad decisions that caused him even more pain.

Being alone can be very therapeutic. To enjoy one's own company is to love and appreciate one's self. Being alone gives us time to rest, meditate, read, and nurture ourselves. When we're alone, we have time to enjoy the feeling of God's presence, to pursue our interests and to get to know and appreciate who we are. If you have challenges in spending time alone with yourself, please seriously explore why. If the thought of living alone or spending time alone emotionally triggers you, open your journal now and write down all the feelings you are experiencing. When do you feel lonely? List your fears.

Self-Reflection

I recently attended a gathering where the leader of the group handed us a mirror and asked us to look ourselves in the eye, and then pass the mirror to the next person. It was amazing how many people took the mirror, did not even attempt to look at themselves, and quickly passed the mirror on, often accompanied by uncomfortable laughter.

Go to your mirror now and look yourself in the eye. How does that feel? Can you do it? Can you tell your Soul-self that you love it? What does this bring up for you? Share this experience in your journal.

Sometimes during our infancy and early years, our primary caretakers did not reflect back to us looks of love or words telling us how special we are. We may not have been held or hugged or told we were loved. I was in my early forties when I realized I had no memory of being held affectionately. (I know they carried me from one place to the other, but that's not hugging.) As well, I had no memory of being told that I was loved. I learned later than no one else in our family received any demonstrations of being valued either.

I spent many years trying to get recognition and approval from my mother. The first time I experienced a real compliment from her was when I stopped looking for one.

I remember that day well. I was driving her to a doctor's appointment and mentioned that while she was having her meeting with the doctor, I would sit out front and read the book I brought with me. It was the first time my mother showed interest in my reading, and she asked me what the book was about. I told her it was regarding genetic patterning from the spiritual perspective. I felt she actually heard me, because she turned to me and said, "I'm very proud of you, Judy. Your work must take a lot of focus and energy. It is great that you help so many people." That was the first and only time she complimented me.

Explore your thoughts and possible limitations of self-acceptance. Look into the mirror again. Look directly into your eyes and give yourself *five compliments*. Hear yourself speaking them out loud. Feel the emotions the compliments trigger. Now add the compliments you gave to yourself to your journal entry. Write about how it felt to say them; how it felt to hear them. What came up for you? What was triggered? Allow yourself to process.

What Are Healthy Boundaries?

There is often confusion about what healthy boundaries look and feel like, especially if we were raised in a household without boundaries. Having respect for our own space, thoughts, and feelings, as well as our limitations and needs, is the essence of healthy boundaries. However, these same thoughts and actions must extend out toward others. Having, maintaining, and respecting boundaries works both ways. If we are to respect another person's boundaries, our own boundaries must be healthy.

BETTY

Betty grew up without any demonstrations of healthy boundaries. Her mother insisted that Betty leave the bathroom door open at all times. She was also instructed to leave her bedroom door open so her mother could come and go as she wished.

As Betty grew into a rebellious teenager, she too, lost her boundaries. As an adult, she chose to remove all the interior doors in her home. The doors were a metaphor.

What was created in Betty's life was a huge challenge in respecting others' boundaries, as well as having none of her own. It affected all of her relationships.

How Do Healthy Boundaries Feel?

Healthy boundaries feel empowering. Knowing it is okay and safe to say, "I'm sorry, that doesn't work for me," or, "No, I would rather not be involved," allows you to respect yourself. It is possible to set boundaries without putting up walls.

To respect your own boundaries, it is important to respect your own feelings. Have you ever had someone not take no for an answer and try to talk you into what they want, with no regard for your feelings? Check in with your body to see how you physically feel when your boundaries are being tested. Do you have a knot in the pit of your stomach (your power center)? If so, you may be feeling that you are powerless in the situation. If you feel your throat tighten or have a catch in your throat, this center of communication and choice is blocked, and you fear speaking your truth.

You have the right to say *no*. Learning to say no is your next step in developing healthy boundaries. It may not be easy for you, especially if your parents didn't tolerate it when you were a child. If this feels true for you, document in your journal how your parents taught you this belief.

Remember, no one else can make you feel a feeling. You have choice. If you are in an abusive situation where it is not safe to say no or have your own opinion, please seek help to change those circumstances and to move into your power.

Family members seem to know exactly which buttons to push to bring up uncomfortable feelings, don't they? Have you noticed that your family can trigger you faster than anyone else can? Losing the love of family members is one of the most feared possibilities. We may feel at our most vulnerable around family. When we seek approval and love outside ourselves and our God, we often feel we come up short-changed. We feel loss. We go to fear.

Take in a deep breath and allow the God Energy to fill your lungs. As you exhale, feel the release of fear and discomfort. Each breath you take is God in action. God is constantly demonstrating though us and as us. With each deep breath, feel the unconditional love moving though you and around you. You are not alone. You are love. You are loved.

God does not withhold love because you have your own thoughts and opinions. God does not punish you for your choices. God does not hold grudges and call you names filled with anger and disrespect. God does not judge or criticize you because you are a homosexual, a heterosexual, a bisexual, a Christian, a Pagan, a Buddhist, a Hindu, a Muslim, or an Atheist.

Source always supports us in choice. Source always wants us to be free and happy. When we make poor relationship choices, we have opportunities to learn from our mistakes and make different choices in the future. Nothing is impossible.

Am I Good Enough?

It is such a cliché to blame everything on our childhood, but we cannot discount the effect it has on future relationships.

The lack of self-esteem and self-love is epidemic. We attract the degree and type of relationship based on where we are in our self-love. When fear shows itself as judgment of others, we are really judging ourselves and projecting that onto someone else. I learned this in an interesting way.

There was a time in my life when I was friends with a person who could not get past their judgments and interpretations of me. They missed who I really was as they projected their self-doubt onto me. It was crazy making as I continually tried to defend myself, express myself, and love myself while I was being overwhelmed by accusations that I was something I was not. This friendship was a catalyst for me to practice building healthier boundaries, self-love, and learning to recognize when it was time to end the drama. Then I had the opportunity to reflect on why I had attracted an unhealthy friendship.

CAROLINE

Caroline shared that her greatest fear is of not being good enough and not being loveable. She went on to say, "I'm afraid I'm not enough. I'm afraid of being wrong, of not being what I 'should' be. Who am I to be loved? Who would want me? Who would want to stay with me?"

We can hear the pain of self-doubt and fear of abandonment in her words.

Find the Truth of who you are. Stay grounded in knowing that God loves you just as you are, no matter what anyone else says or thinks.

I Must Be Perfect to Be Loved

The need to be perfect is self-limiting. Believing we need to be perfect is self-defeating. If we are driven by perfectionism, we are likely attempting to prove to someone that we are good enough. The inner critic tells us lies like, "*You will never be good enough. Who do you think you are? Unless you're perfect, you will never amount to anything. I expect you to perform perfectly, or why bother?*" This self-judgment is the dark ego.

If your parents were critical and judgmental of you when you were a child, it's more than likely that you adopted the perfectionist attitude, *I must be perfect to be loved.* This may also lead you into future relationships with judgmental people. That's a hard and lonely road to walk. I know. I have walked that road many times. I spent many years playing the perfectionist role. Yes, I worried what other people thought about me, and, worse than that, my inner critic drove me crazy with "shoulds." Just being me didn't feel like enough. I felt like I was competing with my in-laws and my friends, but I was really competing with myself.

In my twenties, when I was a young wife and mother, I was a perfectionist in my home. Not only did I work a nine-to-five job, but I always came home from work and not even changing my clothes, I started dinner, served dinner, and cleaned up after dinner. Then after the children and the husband were in bed, I did laundry, packed lunches, and took care of whatever else needed to be done. I was raised during the 1950s when June Cleaver[9] was the role model of homemaker perfection. She wore a dress, high heels, and pearls while doing housework. Ward Cleaver sat and read the newspaper, just like my husband did. On weekends, I scrubbed the house from top to bottom, then cleaned and waxed the kitchen floors on my hands and knees. If that wasn't enough "homework," in my spare time I sewed many of my own clothes, baked, and canned a lot of our food. Yes, I had a lot more energy at that age than I do now, but the urge and need to be perfect was very strong. Criticism from the past was dictating my present.

Love yourself for who you are, not for what someone else thinks you should be. You cannot change other people or what they think of you. But when you change the way you think of yourself, others may change, too. When you

---

9   The mother character from the 1950s television program *Leave It to Beaver*.

forgive yourself for your imperfections, you will forgive and be much kinder to others for theirs. God does not judge us. God does not criticize us. God believes we are already perfect in our imperfection and in who we are right now. Limited thinking keeps us from being the magnificent Being we truly are, our God-self.

Take a moment to write down all the ways your inner perfectionist and critic acts out and diminishes you. Then take a deep breath and allow yourself to think about all that is good within you right in this moment. Write that down, too.

Do you hesitate to do this writing? Are you having any challenges in finding your good and claiming your good? What comes up for you? Do you feel the energy of—and the love for—the Soul within you? Write in your journal what you are discovering about yourself. There is no right or wrong. Be kind to yourself. Later in the book, you will experience a powerful release exercise.

JOAN

"Fear is not a disease of the body; fear kills the soul."

—Mahatma Gandhi

When I asked Joan her greatest fear, she replied, "If I am truly whole, healed, and I love myself, I will be alone. I think that if I have my act together, why would anyone want me?" This may sound like a very odd fear. It seems that if we reach this level all would be fine.

But, you see, Joan was raised in a very codependent family. The fixers and caretakers in the family gave Joan a lot of attention when she was practicing her eating disorder. In her love relationships, she attracted the same kinds of caretakers, or she became the caretaker for those who were practicing their own woundedness. She went on to say, "If they have their act together, why would I want them? And why would they want or need my love?"

Joan is insightful and has good awareness of her wrong thinking and attachment, maybe even addiction, to being emotionally wounded. Our dysfunctional thoughts can be familiar and somewhat comfortable. They're also destructive.

But in her attempt to be perfect, Joan was acting out her feelings of unworthiness. As much as she wanted to be loved for who she was, she didn't love herself as she was. Joan shared that she did not believe she was being seen before she began acting out through her disorder. Our work together was to help her find self-love and acceptance inside, not outside, herself. She was in multilevel therapies, which included not only our work together, but also her work with an eating disorder therapist and a nutritionist.

When we don't feel self-respect and self-love, we look outside ourselves for it. We look to others to provide what we feel is missing within us. We may seek this love and approval through addictions such as eating disorders, alcoholism, and drugs. There is an emptiness that we are trying to fill. But no thing can fill it! This is separatist thinking, which we are often taught in religion. When we believe that God is out there in a church somewhere, or up in the clouds, instead of within us, we are involved in separatist thinking. But when we discover the Truth that God is within us, that *God is the very life that is us*, we have the key to finding love for ourselves within ourselves.

In seeking relationships, people are often looking to be loved for the wrong reasons. They may look at being loved as a fix-all. Do you think that if you find someone to love you, you will be happy? No one else can make you happy. Do you think that if you just love your spouse enough, that your spouse will be well, happy, and whole? We cannot make someone else feel loved. Love is a gift we must first give to ourselves and then we can give it to others. And when we love ourselves, receiving another person's love is a precious gift.

Play along with me here. If you were a cake, what kind of cake would you be? If you have created your self-cake with a lot of self-love, honor, and self-respect, you are a darn fine cake and can stand on your own. Love from others is just the icing on the top. We all want to be loved, accepted, and appreciated. Moving into self-love and acceptance is the key to experiencing more joy. How we intrinsically treat ourselves is how we will treat others. Subconsciously we will attract people to us that will treat us the way we treat ourselves. As Oprah says, "We teach others how to treat us."[10] So absolutely true.

Own the truth of who you really are. The Source of All That Is knows the Truth of who you really are. The Source

---

10   Oprah Winfrey, television producer/host, *Oprah's Life Class*, Oprah Winfrey Network, June, 2012.

knows your talents, your possibilities, and sees your light within. Allow the light within you to shine forth through your thoughts, words, and feelings. No matter what ego tells you, *you can control your words, your feelings, and your thoughts.* You always have choice.

Use your red stop light to block the negative thoughts and fill the silence with a deep, purifying breath. Strongly speak this affirmation to yourself: *I am a child of the Divine, and I deserve the very best. I am filled with gratitude, knowing that with my talents I serve the world. I forgive myself for any mistakes I have made, and I move forward in my knowing the Truth of who I am and that the energy of the One Source moves through me, filling every cell of my body, as me.*

Guided Meditation #2

(I suggest you record this meditation.)

Sit back, deep into your chair, in a comfortable position, and feel yourself being supported by a loving energy holding you safely and securely. Take a deep, cleansing breath, the breath of life, God's Life Force. Feel it move deeply into your lungs, radiating out, into, and through every cell of your body.

With each deep breath, allow yourself to relax more, as your muscles let go of all stress and tension.

When you are ready, gently direct your mind to a beautiful green meadow. The many wildflowers are colorful and fragrant. Everything is in full bloom, and the only effect it has on you is one of deep calm and connection to the One energy that contains everything new and all of completion at the same time. Your deep understanding is that all is in Divine order. Let go and trust. As you wander through this healing meadow, you discover a small bamboo bridge over the bluest pond you have ever seen. Leaving your belongings beside the foot of the bridge, step forward onto the bridge. You notice a beautiful energy. Midway over the bridge, stand still. You are not sure of what you are seeing, or feeling, but you become aware of an ethereal Being.

Take another deep breath, letting go of the busy mind. Just allow yourself to feel the gentle, loving energy that is emanating from this One.

It turns to you and holds out Its hand. Without hesitation, you take the hand offered, and this simple touch takes you deeper into your centeredness than you have ever been before. By allowing this shift, you hear Its words:

Welcome, dear one, to this bridge between your past and your potential. You have choice to leave behind your stories and to create new experiences. You have choice to move away from the pain and suffering and move into the Truth of who you are. Yes, this means change for you. You have choice now to release your fears and take a step forward into that which is awaiting your discovery.

Before you stepped onto this bridge, you left all that no longer serves you behind. If you choose to turn back and pick up what you released, you may do so. You will not be doing anything wrong. If you choose to walk forward, over the bridge into the unknown, I will hold your hand along each step of your journey. Of course, there will be life's challenges, opportunities, and choices on the new path. Please know that your next step is always a new step and will be exactly as you see it to be. However, you are never alone.

What do you choose?

You realize you forgot to breathe. Take a deep breath. You know in your heart what it is you feel you need to do. Decide what direction you want to go. Feel free to ask this Guide questions and receive answers. This is your private time. When you feel complete, make your decision. Take this moment to share your decision with this loving Being. Then move into the direction you have chosen.

You discover that the Holy One is by your side to walk with you, whatever direction you have chosen. You realize you are not alone and never have been.

When you finish your process, leave the bridge. Not far ahead of you is a bench. Sit there and get your bearings. Go to your heart center and rest your hands there, allowing your awareness of strong spiritual connection to flow over your physical body and at the same time, into and through your Soul.

There is warmth in your Soul. Acknowledge the Soul that is within this physical shell known as you. Feel your inner light radiating forth. Allow yourself to feel merged with the light of your guidance, this consciousness that walks your path with you.

Now, take another deep, centering breath and bring the awareness with you as you once again become aware of your physical body and your surroundings on the Earth.

BREATHE. Take this opportunity to journal your experience of this meditation and the choices you made.

Affirmational Prayer

I am aware at all times of the magnificent presence of the Mother, Father, God, Goddess in my life. Every breath I take is God in form. The Source IS all there IS. I know the Truth that this presence moves through me, as me. I embrace change as I breathe into the knowing that I AM ONE with the Divine Energy.

My intention is to release all attachments, issues, fears, and blocks that keep me from moving forward on my Soul's path. I know the Truth of my Divinity. Source, I know I am in Your safekeeping and that only the best is here for me now.

As I hold you in my heart and know you will never abandon me, I release my fears of abandonment and aloneness. No matter what the outward appearances are, I am never alone. I accept the Universal support, as I eagerly take steps to change my life and move forward with ease and grace. I know I am safe in Your Keeping as I journey into the unknown and enjoy life's adventures.

I embrace the change that brings me opportunity and growth. I give unending thanks as I release this knowing into Universal Law for complete manifestation. I am so grateful and so blessed!

And so it is. Amen.

RELATIONSHIPS SEEK THEIR OWN LEVEL

So What Are You Afraid Of?

Not only relationships with others, but first our relationships with our Source and our self are also crucial to our personal growth. What are you bringing to the relationship table? Blaming others for things that happen to you is a waste of energy and opportunity for personal growth. I cannot stress enough the importance of taking responsibility for your own behavior. No one else is responsible for your actions, your thoughts, your words, your happiness, your feelings, or your actions. If you are still blaming your parents, your siblings, your children, your husband, your wife, boss, friend, exes, the government, ethnic groups, or anyone else for ruining your life, then it's time to release and let go of this negative thinking.

Some people don't want to believe they have choice in their life. They are in denial, in fear of taking responsibility for their perceptions. They think if they have choice that it means they have chosen self-punishment, guilt, and victimhood. Well, yes, they actually have chosen this road subconsciously. In so many words, they claim to be powerless. But no one else can make us feel anything.

When we take full responsibility for where we are in our lives, in this very moment, without blaming anyone else, we are empowered. Of course, challenging things still happen to "good" people. What happens to you does not make you either "good" or "bad." If you don't like how your life and your relationships are turning out, you can make a conscious choice to view things differently from this moment forward. If you don't like the world as it appears to you, change the way you look at the world.

LOUISE

Twenty-five years ago, Louise divorced her fifth husband, Paul. Today, if his name comes up, she still moves into accusations, blame, and tears. "It's entirely his fault," she always says. But she says the same thing about the reasons behind the first four divorces. She does not take responsibility for her part in the demise of any of her marriages. She doesn't see that her controlling and manipulative behavior, created by her victim mentality, drove her five husbands away. She has family members who have also been hurt by her bad behavior. She wonders why they don't visit her or call her anymore.

At seventy-eight, Louise still talks about her abusive childhood and her terrible siblings. She blames her adult children for not loving her enough and not visiting her. She does not understand that the lies she has told her children are what have torn the family apart. Louise has sabotaged all her familial relationships. After years of not seeing that she was creating her own reality and negative karma by her negative words, behaviors, thoughts, and actions, Louise is unhappily alone, unhealthy, miserable, and still not choosing to change.

We cannot change or learn anything new from the old negative beliefs we still carry. *Everything revolves around change.* We must change in order to grow. We must change in order to have different experiences. We must change in order to have different relationships. And we must let go in order to change. For a conversion from the mind to the soul, we must move into change.

Relationships give us the opportunity to learn about ourselves. We have choices to grow from our experiences or stay stuck in who we are, blame our partners, and continue to attract the same type of relationships. You may have heard yourself say, "I'm never going to get into another relationship. There are no good men/women out there."

But when you change, other people also seem to change. When you heal your wounded-ness, you attract a different kind of relationship. It will seem as if all your relationships are changing. We know that water seeks its own level. Relationships do, too.

ROBERT

Robert was quick to judge others and jump into anger if they had characteristics that he didn't like. What was happening, of course, was that these people were reflecting back to him characteristics about himself that he hated. Robert would pick a fight or create drama, blame his anger on others, and then use their arguing back as an excuse to "never talk to them again." One day an old friend, a woman he had sworn to never speak to again, was found dead in her bathroom by her family. When Robert learned of her sudden death, he was shocked. He suddenly had a deep awareness of how small the issues were for which he had judged his friend. He went into deep grief for his loss, but even more grief for the loss his friend's family was experiencing. He went into compassion.

Robert knew he had to forgive himself for the anger and judgment he carried toward his "life-path teacher," who through her death had taught him forgiveness.

Commitment

What is commitment? Webster's Dictionary gives this definition: "to entrust."[11] I think the word also means "To keep a promise."

Fear of commitment may lead to self-sabotage. If we

---

11   *Merriam-Webster Dictionary*, Kent, UK: Bell Publishing, Ltd., 2005.

don't keep promises to ourselves and others, we will lose respect for ourselves and *from* others. When respect is lost, loss of love is not far behind. Loss of self-respect leads to inner pain. Inner pain usually leads to a Band-Aid cure, which is usually an addiction of some kind.

How do you feel about keeping a commitment or promise to yourself, a friend, or a loved one? How do you feel about committing to a relationship? Committing to marry? Committing to volunteering in your spiritual community or serving those in need? Journal your thoughts about these issues and any triggers that may come up for you.

If we view promises as sacred commitments to our self and others, we may be more able to keep them. Don't make commitments if you cannot keep them.

Comparing humanness to Godliness, let us remember the promises of love and protection God made to us and has kept. If we stay in faith of this Truth, we will feel ourselves in God's care. If we believe the lies the dark ego tells us, such as God's promises are not kept, we will turn our back on the commitments and promises we have made. If we commit to walking the path our Master Teachers have walked, all of our commitments will unfold within us and through us.

Our greatest commitment is to be present in our relationship with our God. Keeping a commitment to ourselves, our personal growth path, our relationships, and how we serve others in our community will bring peace within.

Loyalty

Loyalty is a fine human quality. I believe in loyalty. To whom and to what are you loyal? If you're loyal to ego, abuse, negativity, users, and cheaters, you need to change. If you find you're defending an abusive situation, seek help. Do not let fear keep you loyal to someone or something that is taking your power away. Misplaced loyalty can harm yourself and others.

To whom have you been loyal in your life? Were they, or are they, really worthy of your loyalty? Make a list in your journal of those you felt loyalty to, and after each name document whether they deserved it or not, as you see it now through the eyes, knowledge, and heart of an adult.

ROGER

Roger was not loyal to his family. They were very good to him, but, unfortunately, he was self-serving and easily took sides against those who stood by him. It was said, in fact, that his loyalty lies with the "highest bidder." Instead of being present for his loved ones, he treated them as though they were unworthy; as though he didn't trust them. Sometimes he even defended strangers instead of them.

After Roger had a stroke, his son took him into his home. Family members kept in touch and helped in all ways possible. But Roger's passive-aggressive behavior and manipulation often triggered his adult children into guilt, followed closely by resentment. He often ridiculed his family behind their backs and insinuated that he was being mistreated. At first believing him, his family began to blame one another. They expressed hurt and confusion as they witnessed a lack of loyalty in the family dynamics. After finally sharing upsetting stories with one another, however, they figured out it was their father who was behind the dissention.

Roger's family felt they were worthy of their father's love, loyalty, and respect, but they were confused as to why he didn't think they were worthy. They eventually remembered what their father had told them his childhood had been like. They began to think they could understand how and why he did not demonstrate loyalty. Roger had never had a role model for love, loyalty, or respect.

Roger's father was a bootlegger in the 1920s. He was an alcoholic who lied, cheated, and evaded his taxes. He was a womanizer and often had irate husbands chasing after him. He was also abusive to his wife and children. Roger's mother defended her abusive husband and made no effort to rescue her son or his siblings from their father's violent, alcoholic rage. (Due to his addictions, Roger's father died in his forties.) Loyalty to the children was never shown in Roger's childhood. His parents always took the side of whoever had the money or the power. Their children, Roger included, always felt betrayed and minimized.

Closeness

When we are in a relationship, we may see our loved one's fears through their behaviors, but we may not identify the fear within ourselves. If you fear closeness and intimacy, you may draw relationships with other people who also fear closeness and deep intimacy.

Are you familiar with the dance of intimacy? You've probably danced it many times. When we come together at the beginning of a relationship, we are both literally and metaphorically standing face-to-face. Let's pretend your partner, who wants to be closer, takes the first step toward you. But you may become uncomfortable, so you take a step backward. Your partner, who wants to discuss his or her needs, keeps stepping forward. You keep moving back, but then maybe you process what's happening. Maybe you work through a layer of fear and decide, okay, you'll take a chance and move to the next level. That's when you stop backing up. Maybe you even take a baby step forward as you accept more connection. But now your partner starts backing up! He or she starts shutting down, going to their own level of fear. Your partner may stop dead in their tracks. Wanting more, you push forward. At some point, the other person may become comfortable and think, *What the hell, let's give it a go.* He or she takes a step forward...and you go to fear again and withdraw. Get the picture? The dance of intimacy has moved into full swing.

Dating unavailable people who are married or otherwise committed is a sure sign of your fear of true intimacy and commitment. Do you blame your partner for lack of commitment, closeness, sensitivity, and abandonment? If they do not act out the relationship fears, you will.

Are you a runner? Do you know what I mean by that? A runner is the one who bales out when things get rough. The runner is the one who shuts down, checks out, withdraws, and ends the relationship before its time. Sound familiar?

ROSALIE

Rosalie came to a session with me to work on health and relationship issues. She has been in a thirty-year relationship with a married man. It was her fear of commitment and intimacy that created the attraction of this dysfunctional relationship.

Now, at the age of sixty-five, she is facing her retirement years as a single woman who chose to never experience a committed relationship. Rosalie chose to never marry, never have children. Well, with those choices, she doesn't have to worry about abandonment, does she? I'm not saying she isn't happy or that she made the wrong choices. What I'm saying is that now she gets to look at the choices she made and take responsibility for any hidden fears that have created her health issues and her dysfunctional relationships.

Every choice has a consequence. If we take responsibility for our choices, and stop blaming others for what we think is their "inability to be present and make a commitment," we can stand in our Truth of who we are and move forward to heal the wounds that create our negative experiences.

Generational Beliefs

How your parents and grandparents felt about their personal love relationships and how they handled major challenges affect you. What your parents, for example, witnessed between their parents is likely to be what they demonstrated to you. Are you bringing forward into your relationships old issues you witnessed in your parents' relationship dynamic?

My mother was married and divorced three times, but I never heard her take responsibility for her part in the ending of the marriages. She did often tell me how terrible men are. How could those lessons possibly help me in my future relationships? In spite of what I was taught, however, I must say I had many good relationships with men. I like men. But the real issue isn't about the gender, is it?

Did your parents display affection toward each other? Did you hear them say they loved each other? Did they respect each other? Did they respect their relationship?

We have a choice to continue to believe what our parents told us about relationships or we can choose to think differently. Holding on to the negative belief systems we were taught will not help us have healthy relationships. This is one of those areas where you can examine the beliefs you were given and decide whether you want to release any that don't make sense to you..

Open your journal and list what you remember of overt or covert demonstrations by your primary caretakers on how to be in and with relationships. Reread what you have written. How much have you copied from what your parents demonstrated? Decide what you want to release and make a conscious decision to let go of anything that no longer serves you. Keep this promise to yourself. *You are worth the effort of change.*

Engulfment

Engulfment shows itself as a feeling of being suffocated or closed in on. I remember a new relationship many years ago, in which I explained that I was only willing to cuddle for a few minutes and would then be going to "that chair over there" to get some space. At that time, I felt very uncomfortable if there was too much physical contact. Was that a red flag, or what! That relationship was a gift to me because I was able to work on healing my fear of intimacy and engulfment issues. In my next relationship, I was able to stay present emotionally and physically. Hallelujah!

Engulfment certainly includes the fear of vulnerability. How can a relationship thrive or grow if we cannot stand still and be vulnerable with our partner? When we fear being vulnerable, we are not in trust that we are safe. We may feel hurt, rejection, betrayal or, of course, abandonment.

Vulnerability

Vulnerability, in a love relationship, is a necessary area to explore. When we allow our self to be vulnerable in an intimate relationship, we are opening our heart and trusting our partner. As the American poet Theodore Roethke said, "Love is not love until love is vulnerable."[12] When we are still carrying the fears and pain of the past in our heart, our heart will harden and no one will be able to get in. When this emotional hardening happens and the wall is up, we truly are not allowing a powerful, healthy relationship to grow and blossom.

When we share our feelings with our loved one, coming from a trust that they will not judge us, this can help our relationship grow. Everyone expresses in a different way. Allow your partner to have his or her own expression. So often, there is the expectation of how our partner should think, be, and express. We create blocks in communication by allowing our inner critic (the ego) to clutter up our mind with judgment and negativity.

God is our greatest support, greatest connection, and greatest relationship if we will allow ourselves to trust and be vulnerable. You may be hearing the negative self-talk: *Why should I trust God? I have been let down too many times. God does not give me what I want. I continue to have struggles. I do not feel a connection to God. I do not think God even listens to me. I don't know if God even exists.* It does not really matter if these beliefs were taught to you by

---

12   *The Collected Poems of Theodore Roethke,* Anchor Books, 1975.

your primary caretakers, triggered by a negative religious experience, or created by a tragedy. They are false teachings and demonstrations of fear.

We may say similar things about our relationships with people. I think it's interesting that our relationships with our Source, with our self, and with others are all interconnected. They reflect onto one another. We must seek balance in these areas to enjoy harmony in our lives.

You may need to take a great big breath and jump into the vulnerability. Open your journal and write your feelings about being vulnerable. When you're ready, try sitting down with your partner to share and discuss these feelings. Move into trust that your partner may also carry some of the same concerns. Ask them and give them time and space to share how they feel about this issue.

Communication

One of the greatest challenges we human beings have is communication. Look at the condition of relationships in the world—personal, political, and religious. If we all speak from our inner baggage, we are truly limited, and no one understands anyone else. We may have challenges not only expressing our thoughts but also hearing the other person's viewpoint. Think about our interpretations of another person's tone of voice, facial expressions, eye movements, body language, and hand gestures. How and what do these demonstrations communicate to us?

Add to this the many electronic communication tools that eliminate, or at least diminish, real human contact. Consider emailing, social networking, social media, and texting, to name a few. I use email for scheduling and business interactions. I use social networking for limited interactions. But I refuse to text, preferring to use the telephone. I want to hear the person's tone of voice, and I want them to hear mine.

BEN AND HATTIE

This husband and wife were not on stable ground to begin with—and then they began texting their arguments to one another. When I asked them why they didn't use their cell phones to call each other instead of texting, they blamed each other, saying their partner refused to talk on the cell. Neither would commit to stop texting. Their relationship was filled with tremendous drama that was compounded by misinterpretations of their text messages.

Texting instead of talking, blaming, and misreading each other's intentions destroyed their relationship. Ben and Hattie had eliminated the most important elements of their communication—voice, eye contact, body language, and touch.

It's said that the eyes are the windows to the soul. How often do you look into the eyes of your loved one, especially when there is discontent? Ben and Hattie never looked into each other's eyes. They didn't have any healthy contact with one another when they shot text messages back and forth.

When we do not acknowledge our Soul or the Soul in the other, we cannot feel our Oneness.

Interactive Listening

Listening is a talent. Do you sit in silence as your partner or friend shares his or her thoughts and ideas with you? Or do you sit with your mind running and planning what brilliant reply you will make? Active listening is important for productive communication.

Because what you say and what people hear is not always the same thing, it is important to clarify what is being shared. To do this, listen, then repeat back to your partner what you thought you heard him or her say and get confirmation or correction before you take your turn in sharing your thoughts. Remember to look into your partner's eyes as you speak.

There is quite a difference between reacting and responding. When we hear something that pushes our button, we may have an unthinking reaction and speak from a negative place and in a negative way. Instead of reacting, take a deep breath and notice what part of your body you feel discomfort in. Take a moment to collect this internal information and respond in a non-defensive manner. This takes practice, of course, so you can practice in every conversation you have with anyone.

When we (or others) come from fear and hurt, we may not clearly hear the other person's words or the meaning behind their words. We may react in old patterns of defensiveness and throw attacking, angry words toward our loved ones. Our reactions or responses need to be consciously chosen. We can only be in charge of the words that come out of our mouths. Your anger hurts you much worse than you realize. What you hold within you moves outward into your life.

Both people in a conversation need to participate in active listening skills. It is not difficult, it's just different. You will be exercising new "muscles." Practice patience with yourself and your partner. Always make sure ego is not filling your mind with negative thoughts. Observe, listen, and stop any negative, destructive thoughts before they come out of your mouth.

What Is Resignation?

By now, you are aware that I like to use the dictionary. Webster defines "resign" as "to relinquish formally; to give up."[13] I find the phrase "to give up" to be a negative thought in our society. I would prefer to think that there comes a time when we decide to stop being present for what no longer serves us. But that does not mean we are giving up in the passive sense.

What is enough? Each of us chooses when enough is enough. But how long should it take to make that choice? There is no right or wrong amount of time for us to discover we have reached our limit in a situation.

---

13   *Merriam-Webster's Dictionary* (Kent, UK: Bell Publishing, Ltd., 2005).

In years past, I spent much longer deciding to leave a negative situation than I do today. I would stay past a time that was reasonable for me because I feared being judged a quitter. Or I feared an unknown future. Indecision kept me stuck and very stressed.

When, therefore, is it time to move away from the current condition or circumstance and move into something else? Pay attention to what you see around you and feel inside. There are people that come from a negative mind-set. As they pontificate and chew holes in the threads of Light Consciousness, there is no place around them for your Light Being to shine. Check within yourself. How are you feeling about the situation? Are you feeling any emotional or physical pain? Are you experiencing negativity? Do you feel it is time to change? Sometimes we don't think it's possible for something better to come into our life. Maybe you're afraid of how you will look to others when you say, "No more."

Stay in the Light. The dark ego energy may have you doubting yourself and keeping yourself in the dark. Take the first step out of the dark and ask yourself, *What can I learn here? What in this situation will help me grow?* Once we learn the lesson, we don't have to stay in the old pattern. We can work on a new lesson somewhere else. Consciously choose a different outcome if the situation appears again. Recognize the signs of negativity and know that you do not have to keep reliving it.

We can stomp around in anger, we can moan and groan over the condition, but does that change anything?

No. We can deny our conditions, put our heads in the sand, and ignore the challenge. We can say that popular cliché, "It is what it is." But does that change anything? No. We cannot change anyone else, we know that. Therefore, we get to change ourselves from the inside out. If we want to experience something different, we can choose to do and be something different. By being true to ourselves, we can learn to say no faster and more often.

Remember, we have a choice. We can stay stuck in a challenge. We can continue to feel like our energy is being sucked out of us. Or we can move on. Some people carry belief systems that say that it's okay to stay where you are. Well, yes, if that's what you believe, then that is what is right for you at this time. You may not know any different. You may not perceive yourself as stuck. The moment you awaken to the fact that where you are is not serving you, God, or others, then maybe it's time to do something different.

When we resign ourselves to the reality that we are not moving forward—that we are not helping our community move forward—that's when we probably need to move into change.

A few years ago, an opportunity came to me to serve in a community of like-minded people. After about six months of involvement, however, I realized that we really were not that like-minded, after all. I was not there to change them, so I chose to move on and find a new environment that could take me to a greater level of awareness in my personal growth and service to my Source. I knew I was spiritually led when I felt the inner peace.

As you strive to grow, change, and learn, you must look at the people you choose to have in your life. If you are not experiencing inspirational role modeling from them, it may be time to choose new friends and acquaintances. If you're the only one in the group or relationship holding the greater consciousness, you may begin to feel like you're dragging a truckload of negative energy behind you. Unhook that truck! Free yourself to discover how wonderful you are. Do not try to fix other people. Work on yourself. And, by all means, journal, journal, journal.

Personal Power and Our Sense of Self

Has someone given you the responsibility for making him or her happy? Here's the good news: no matter how hard we try, we cannot make another person happy. If they don't want to be happy, they won't be happy.

Don't swim in someone else's pool of chaos, drama, and negativity. Take responsibility for your own behavior, your own happiness, and your own choices. That's when you can be peaceful in the midst of chaos. You can be joyful in the midst of negativity. Do not give your joy away. You need to examine, however, why you spend time in negative relationships, negative work environments, and negative social situations.

Are you a thermometer or a thermostat? A thermometer *reflects* the temperature in the room, that is to say, to its energy and belief systems (negative or positive). A thermostat *changes* the temperature and the energy, in the room. Do you bring positive change into your relationships and environment, or are you part of the problem?

Negative thinking limits our potential. When you are in fear, you are not living in love energy. Ego demonstrates fear and negativity. It is impossible to be happy and negative at the same time.

Spirit does not come from negative thoughts. Pay attention to the "temperature" around you. Be responsible for your own behavior and actions. No one else is responsible, no matter how much you may try to make them be. If you are blaming someone else for your circumstances, you're demonstrating your negative ego-self.

Choose to be a *thermostat* in every situation that needs it.

I'm Not Happy!

Are you free or are you a prisoner of your belief systems regarding relationships? Do you believe that your happiness is the responsibility of your partner? I repeat: *No one else is in charge of your happiness, nor can they possibly make you happy if you don't want to be.* What drama do you create in your relationship? What you believe, you create. If there is a part of you that feels you do not deserve a happy relationship, you will not have one. Examine your beliefs.

Your reactions in a relationship may be coming from your subconscious. That's why you do not understand why you are behaving as you are. You may still be living in past relationship challenges and doubting you can let go of what was.

Do you believe that you deserve better? It is important to communicate with your partner in a positive way. Identify your feelings. If your negative thinking and words stir up trouble...this is your ego talking. It may want to trigger your partner's ego and start a big fight. Egos love to fight. Just look at this world.

Pay close attention to your thoughts, your feelings, and the words you speak to yourself and to your significant other. If these thoughts don't serve you, it's definitely time to release them before fears replace happiness in your relationship. Recognizing and stopping the ego takes awareness and patience. Take a step at a time. Be persistent.

Deeply consider the ideas of reactions and inner feelings. Write your thoughts and realizations in your journal.

Fun and Playtime

What are your feelings about being playful and having childlike fun? Do you feel uncomfortable and silly? If your spouse is playful, do you feel it's a waste of time? Do you want him or her to be more serious?

Remember when you first met your loved one? Remember the first glimpse you had of their magical light within? What part of them were you attracted to? Did you know it was their true self? Maybe you didn't know what it was, but you felt pulled to something special.

Typically, when we meet someone to whom we are very attracted, there is an inner child aspect of ourselves that is triggered. We have strong feelings in our heart chakra, our heart center. We may call it joy, love, glee, playfulness, even youthfulness. That part of us has come "alive" again. What better gift can we give ourselves, and our mate, than to keep that part of us alive? Make a commitment to love this magical, loving part of yourself and your partner.

We have lots of excuses, like busy lives, stress, and responsibilities, that can overpower our thoughts of fun and joy and push aside this valuable inner light. Worse, we may disown this childlike part of our personality and treat ourselves as though our magical self is not important any longer. When we honor all parts of ourselves as God shining through us, we will feel self-love.

If we feel imprisoned by negative thinking and believe our relationships cannot improve—that we are stuck in a nonproductive dead-end job, a loveless marriage, a hopeless health challenge, or even self-hate—then it's time to change the negative pattern of creating endless, end-to-end dramas.

Use your STOP light technique. After strongly affirming STOP to the negative mind chatter, fill your newfound silence with self-loving thoughts and words. Yes, you can do it.

Ask yourself, *What do I need to do to be free from the negative beliefs?* Build your vision. Take a risk. Imagine and dream something better. Make a choice, say a prayer, create a dream. Take action and BELIEVE.

Optimism

I was born an optimistic person. That does not mean that the negativity in the world does not affect me, but I understand that I have a choice to be optimistic or pessimistic. I choose the higher road. I like the view up here better.

Here's my thinking on optimism. I believe that optimism is God talking to us. That small, still voice that tells the Truth. God does not tell us that we should or should not do anything. God does not tell us we are bad or instill fear in us. God does not say negative things to us. When we hold hope in our very core, there is room for God-talk to enter our hearts and speak to us. Source reminds us of our Divine Truth all the time. Are you listening? Or do you go back into doubt and fear? God never deserts us. We desert God.

It is our individual responsibility to keep the negative voice quiet. When negativity overshadows "positivity" and tells us that we cannot have what we want, that we don't deserve the best life has to offer, that we don't deserve our good, that's when it's time to observe these egoic thoughts, pull up the STOP light image in your mind's eye, and again shout, "Stop! Go away! I am not going there with you! I am Love, and I am Loved. I deserve all the blessings of the Universal Kingdom! I believe, and I receive all God's abundance Now! I AM a beloved child of the Universe, and I am grateful for this knowing!"

Staying in optimism is staying in and standing with

Source. God is increase, not decrease. Feel yourself shift. Allow this change to happen. Feel your power. Feel good.

Whatever You Want, Claim It Now

Pay attention to your thoughts, your words, and your feelings, for they express your beliefs. Although we may think that God's energy is invisible, it is visible in everything on this planet. Besides in nature, humans, and animals, God's energy is displayed through the things that we create through our creative mind and then our hands. From the very first shelter a human being created for protection, to the most sophisticated electronic device we have today, it was first a thought with God's energy in it. God created the person who created the thing; therefore, everything is God in form. Including you and me.

Your manifesting power resides in your thoughts, words, and feelings. You may think and believe that these actions would be invisible, but this is far from the Truth. Everything is created from the invisible. Thought is invisible until you think it; words are invisible until you speak them; and feelings are invisible until you feel them. This book was invisible until I put in on paper. My thoughts, words, and feelings come first, and from that energy, which is one with God's energy, I create.

What you believe is NOT invisible, for it is showing up in your life right now. If you don't like what you're manifesting in your life, it's time to change your thoughts, words, and feelings. These changes will then change your life experience.

The Universe always says, "Yes." You are manifesting every moment, either consciously or subconsciously. God does not judge. Old religious beliefs may have taught you that God condemns, judges, and punishes. This is a lie. The dark side of humankind condemns, judges, and punishes, not our Source. God grants our every thought, our every word, our every feeling, according to our core beliefs. What a wonderful gift this is. Our responsibility is to monitor our thoughts, our words, and our feelings.

So are you optimistic or pessimistic? Positive or negative? When you're ready, open your journal and write about your beliefs, thoughts, words, and feelings as they come up for you. It's time to release those negative and pessimistic thoughts. Stop the ego from repeating them to you by using your STOP light tool. Fear, doubt, and worry will create more fear, doubt, and worry. Where you put your energy and attention will be your reality. The Truth within, is where your inner power resides.

Remember Louise from earlier in this chapter? Louise went through many relationships, always recreating the same reality for herself. She found fault with each husband. She called each of her five husbands by many names—lazy, cheap, messy, weak, noisy, and on and on. Guess what? Each husband appeared to her exactly the way she thought of him and labeled him. She created her own reality. That does not mean that the men truly had the characteristics she assigned to them. It means she carried her anger and self-loathing into her relationships, and her judgments played out for her in her experiences.

Of course, the men also chose Louise to play out their dramas of criticism and judgment. Let us hold positive thoughts for these men that they learned from Louise and made better choices in their future relationships. As of today, however, it appears that Louise has not yet changed her thinking or her behavior.

It's never too late, never impossible to change if you want to change. Make a decision to accept the Truth of who you are. Are you Spirit having a human experience or a spiritual experience? As you connect to your Higher Self, you have the ever-present possibility of healing and discovering your wholeness within.

Life is one big experience that is constantly changing. When you construct fear-based blocks, you are narrowing your chances of receiving the good you want in your life. You are narrowing your vision and your possibilities. The Truth is that the Universe always wants you to be happy, healthy, and abundant. You need to change and get out of your own way if you want to receive this goodness.

You may not have control, but you certainly have choice. You can choose to see the unknown as an exciting opportunity to create something new. Make a choice to think, feel, speak, and act from positive energy. If you are not disciplined in your thought-life, you will never have the life you want.

On a deep subconscious or emotional genetic level, you may doubt your worthiness to create a fulfilling life. Fear of the unknown and the future will not allow you to create a wonderful now. Did your parents feel they deserved goodness in their lives? Did they allow themselves to fully receive their happiness, radiant health, and abundance?

My parents did not. They didn't know how. Their parents didn't know how, and their parents' parents didn't know how, either. My family history is filled with overwhelming fear, anxiety, depression, suicide, disease, poverty, lies, imprisonment, adultery, molestation, and dysfunctions of every kind. This doesn't mean it has to continue into future generations. Each of us has the ability and the opportunity to move into choice of change. Don't live someone else's stories or your own old ones anymore.

If there are areas in your life that don't work for you, choose change. That famous thinker, Anonymous, once said "We change for two reasons. Either we learn enough that we want to or we've been hurt enough that we have to." When you allow change to enter your life, you won't be sorry. Trust that you will not be going into something worse. Trust that you will be guided to the next step on your healing path. Trust that you will be led to your good. And always remember that God has your back. Even if your own mother and father rejected you, remember God already accepts you as Its very own beloved child. Know you are God's favorite child.

All her life my mother told me overtly or covertly that my youngest brother was her favorite child. It wasn't his fault that she demonstrated and declared her feelings of preference. I was never upset or jealous of my baby brother. But I always had a knowing, even as a young child, that it was strange and inappropriate for my mother to show me, and tell me, that she had a favorite child. As I look back on my childhood, I am very grateful that I had a rather mature knowing and understanding of the challenged thinking and choices the adults in my family acted out.

When I learned that "I am God's favorite child;" Wow, did that feel good. I felt special, and I still do every time I remind myself of this fact. I want you to feel special, too. Memorize this Truth, *I am God's favorite child!* and repeat it to yourself often. The difference between God having a favorite child and my mother having a favorite child is that God sees and treats us all equally. My mother was partial and judgmental.

When you release old teachings, negative inner chatter, and mind clutter and learn how to fully connect spiritually and understand and know the Truth of who you are as a child of the Source, then you move into self-love and feeling loved by the Universe. Then, and only then, can you truly receive your full abundance, health, and happiness.

I Have a Gift for You

The gift is the knowing that you get everything you think, feel, and say. The Universe always says, "Yes." Think about this: You don't get what you ask for, you don't get what you pray for, you get what you believe.

No one can steal this gift from you. You may choose to give it away. You may choose to ignore it. You may deny it. If you do not believe this Truth, look at why you don't believe. List your reasons for not believing. What do you believe? Don't blame others for your lack of self-worth. If you choose to live your life as a victim, the Universe says *okay*, and—*presto!* There you are, experiencing your life as a victim. But if you choose to live your life in peace (no matter what the outer chaos may be), mindfulness, compassion, and awareness, the Universe says *okay* again, and—*Presto!* Your life is what you, again, believe.

When we give up being responsible for our own lives, our own decisions, our own happiness, our own health, and our own prosperity, we start blaming others for taking those things away. The Truth is that our challenge is not about the other person. Take responsibility for your life. Practice change every day.

OLGA

Olga is one of angriest women you could ever meet. She blames everyone on the planet for the challenges in her life. She's one of these road-raging drivers you hear about. She cuts other cars off in traffic and then gives them the famous hand signal of scorn. (You know which one I mean.) She blames the mother that adopted her at birth. She blames the biological mother that gave her away. She blames her ex-husband, her current boyfriend, and all her other friends for every wrong ever done to her. She blames the numerous employers who let her go because she was impossible to tolerate in their workplaces. No matter what happens, she blames the government, her landlord, and her own children. Olga refuses to see her responsibility in anything.

Most of Olga's relationships have walked away from her. The real tragedy is that her two young boys take the brunt of her rage. The fear in their eyes tells the truth about their lives. But we know these wonderful, beautiful young boys have made Soul choices to experience this negativity for a reason. I emphasize "Soul choices" because at a deeper Soul level, each Soul matches itself with a family for its very own Soul path. The human family connection that we choose brings us the gift of growth our Soul seeks. It then follows for every member of the family that each Soul has an opportunity for advancement. I trust that each of us has the perfect primary relationships in our human experience to support our Soul's journey of unfolding into the Truth of our wholeness and Oneness.

With this understanding, we can choose to hold an image in our hearts and in our prayers that these Souls will heal from the verbal abuse and the negative demonstration of what it's like to live in pain and suffering within oneself. God has their backs, understands their challenges, and supports their spiritual growth as they find the path to self-love and forgiveness in spite of their mother and their upbringing. God provides unconditional love to Olga regardless of her behavior and unawareness of her God-self. The Truth is that she can make a choice to change her behavior, her actions, and, therefore, her life.

This gift of holding the Truth of God's love in our heart for others and sending light and healing energy to support them on their Soul's journey is the greatest gift we can give those Souls who have chosen a challenging life. And what

Soul among us has not chosen a challenging life? I am grateful for my life's challenges, for in them I have had my greatest Soul growth.

Are You Authentic?

The older I get, the more authentic friends I have. Maybe this is because *the older I get, the more authentic I am.* I see others differently, because I am different.

Are you living a lie? Are you out of integrity? Are you authentic? Are you true to yourself and others? Or are you only showing your false face? Are you afraid of other people seeing who you really are?

You have an authentic self. It lives within you as the Light of your Spirit. Are you in touch with your Light? Examine where you are in your life. Lies, lack of truth, lack of integrity, and inauthentic behavior all fall under the heading of *fear.* Fear is darkness. Fear will keep you in darkness. Walking into the Light, into the Truth, into the unknown, and into change seems to frighten many people.

Truth will set you free. Integrity, authenticity, and being real are in alignment with the Universe and Love. How bad can that be? Different, yes. Bad? Not at all.

When you love yourself, you are witnessing God within. When you feel God within, you will feel unconditional love. When you feel unconditional self-love, it will be easy to be authentic. Be yourself and allow others to see your God-self.

Guided Meditation #3

(You may want to record this meditation.)

Settle yourself in a comfortable position and take three deep breaths. In your mind's eye, allow yourself to step onto a beautiful path that leads you into a vibrant green meadow. It is peaceful and calm here. The energy feels familiar and loving.

You wander through this space to find a perfect spot to just be still. You may have chosen a shady or sunny spot, it does not matter. You notice a handmade quilt has been laid out for you on the soft grass.

Lie down on the quilt and look up at the blue sky. You notice many clouds drifting by. Some of the clouds are dark, and you wonder if rain is coming. In the clouds, you begin to notice many shapes, symbols, and faces of people who have influenced you in your life. Some of these faces are of people who live in fear and gave you messages based in fear. Gather all the information as it appears to you.

Make a conscious choice right now to disclaim ownership of all the messages that misled you and have kept you in fear. And, as you do so, you see the images in the clouds shifting. One by one, the clouds carrying the dark energy are blown away as a soft breeze moves over you. Let them go. Take your time. Witness all releases completely. Breathe.

Feel the energy shift. Feel yourself become lighter. Notice that the sky is bright now. The dark clouds have passed. The sun is out and shining for you. Feel the love energy surrounding you. When you feel complete and ready, stand with your arms outstretched and give thanks to those who were your teachers. In their own way, they taught you what ego mentality is.

You now know that you always have the power and the knowledge of that energy and can recognize thought patterns that do not serve you. From this day forward, you can make a conscious choice to release negativity as soon as you discover it.

This quilt is a gift to you. Pick it up, wrap it around your shoulders, and feel the Universe hugging you. Feel the warmth, the protection, and the power. Begin your walk back out of the meadow with lightness in your heart center.

Take another deep breath and allow yourself to return to your physical body.

In your journal, list everything you released during this meditation. When you are ready, make a drawing of your magical quilt of love.

Affirmational Prayer

God's presence is here right now. It is in the smallest grain of sand, in the highest star. God's energy is in everything, in everyone, everywhere, all the time. Breathe it in. As I know I am one with Source, I know this Truth for you.

God guides me into the experiences and relationships where I receive my good and my growth. I joyfully move into my creativity and passion for life.

I allow complete health to exist in my body. I allow my purpose to surface into my awareness and show me the best way I can serve others. I move into greater love for others as I move into greater love for myself.

I am so blessed. I am filled with gratitude as I release this blessing into the Universal Law of the One Mind that always says *yes* in the now.

It is done, it is done, it is done. It is so and so it is, Amen.

SURRENDER WHAT?

Fear of Losing Control

Does the thought of losing control send shivers up your spine? Releasing control is one of the most difficult things humans must learn. We carry the illusion that we have control, but the more we struggle to maintain it, the less we have of it. No matter how hard we try, we really don't have control. Ego wants to control. Ego tells you that you must be in control to survive.

Let's look at the connections between fear of the unknown, fear of losing control, and fear of the future. Do you feel out of control if you don't know what's coming next? I had a client who wanted to know exactly what was going to happen in our next session. I couldn't answer that question, of course, because I didn't know what was going to happen in our next session. I explained to her that God is in charge and tells me what to do and when to do it. That's when the miracles happen. But she didn't like this answer because it made her feel out of control. Hence, her work with me around her control issues.

Notice that as soon as you think you have control the Universe shows you how human you are. Let us look at the word *human* as a variation of the word *humiliation,* which often leads us to *humility.* Have you tried to control everything and everyone in your life, only to discover the Universe introduces you to humiliation and soon to humility?

I have a sign on my office wall. I don't know who wrote it or where it came from. It just showed up on my fax machine one day. You may be familiar with the message. *Good morning,* it said, *this is God. I will be handling all of your problems today. I will not need your help. So, relax and have a great day.* I love this message! I repeat it to myself often. It makes me feel lighter when I release control to my Source. Feel free to copy this message and hang it where you can view it and read it to yourself. Enjoy the release to Source.

Anxiety may appear when we feel we have lost the control that we actually never had. We structure our lives with routines, calendars, and schedules so we can feel we have control. But control is an illusion. When that illusion falls apart, we often fall apart.

When asked their greatest fear, many people respond, "I fear loss of control." Some deny their control issues. Others may be told they are controlling, but they just don't see it.

REBECCA

Rebecca, a strong woman who had started her own nonprofit charity and fund-raising business, eventually needed a board of directors. It was not long, of course, before the Universe brought her board members who challenged her. This was Connie, who eventually became the president of the board. She and Rebecca butted heads repeatedly as they mirrored one another's control issues. Their dissention created tension within the organization and among the employees. The challenges from Connie offered Rebecca countless opportunities for introspection as she tried to learn that it was not Connie's challenge, but her own.

Our issues with another person are rarely about the other person. Trying to work (or play) with them, we get to look at our own issues. It wasn't only in the business environment that Rebecca tried to be in control of things. She also tried to control her relationships, and her intensions were good, but she tried so hard to control her family and friends that she actually pushed them away. One of her sisters called her General Rebecca as she tried to make the point that she (Rebecca) was in her control mode again. All the while, Rebecca continued to deny her destructive, controlling behavior.

When we fear life, change, and the unknown, we struggle to stay in control. If you feel anxiety and fear loss of control, take a deep breath and choose to surrender the outcome to the Source of All That Is. Yes, it's as easy as that.

When we realize we are not in control over anything except our own thoughts, perceptions, actions, responses, and choices, *we feel free*. We may have a goal, a responsibility, a job to be done, or a deadline and not know how to make it all happen. God knows the answer and operates in Divine order. As humans, we only see a small part of the whole picture, but our Source knows everything we need and when we need it. This might be an excellent time to go into an intentional prayer of surrender. Here is an effective example:

Divine Source of All That Is, my intention is to meet the goal that has been brought to me. I do not know how it will happen, but I know You do. I surrender all my worries, control, and concerns to You. I know I have been brought onto this journey to serve in this manner for a reason. I release how, when, where, and why this is all to happen. I now turn this situation over to you, knowing the highest good will be the result for all concerned. In gratitude, I say, Amen.

It doesn't matter what our goal or need may be. When we use a prayer of surrender, everything falls into place with ease and grace. When we allow God to be involved, everything is easier. Trusting in an energy greater than ourselves, knowing we will receive a positive outcome— that is where our freedom, power, and peace lie.

I Do NOT Need This Any Longer

When we embrace change, it becomes easier to release and let go of old beliefs. It is also easier to let go of the clutter in all the forms it may demonstrate in your life. You may have been holding on to clutter in the form of beliefs or in the form of the stuff overflowing in your closets. It may be in the form of hanging on to relationships that no longer serve you. Whatever form you choose to clutter up your emotional or physical space, it will block you from receiving your Divine good.

Loss is inevitable. When we hang on to material things for dear life, we set ourselves up for deep, deep stuckness. As difficult as this fact is to face, *everything is temporary. Everything must change.* God created continuous change, as we witness in the cycle of seasons. Mother Earth is always readjusting and shifting Her energies.

Unfortunately, everyone we love must leave. This may be through death, divorce, personal growth, or a move across the country. Nothing remains forever. One of our elusive goals is to keep things from changing. We may feel like a failure when we cannot hold on to everything and never let anything change.

MAGGIE

Maggie complained about her husband's choice of food, books, exercise, supplements, friends, clothing… everything. She complained about her daughter's choice of husband, home, and parenting skills. She complained about her sister's life and her cousin's partner. On and on, Maggie continued criticizing and judging other people's lives.

Focusing on criticizing others was Maggie's distraction

from what was not working in her own life. Her marriage of thirty-six years was in trouble. Her husband, Bruce, said that he felt so belittled and negated that he needed time to rediscover himself. Maggie was thus shocked and devastated when he left her for another woman. She spent months blaming him for all their relationship challenges. It took a long time for her to understand she also had some responsibility in the demise of the marriage.

She was finally able to identify her controlling and critical behavior, the parts of her that caused her pain and difficulty in relationships. She finally learned that others' choices were really none of her business. Becoming aware of her opportunities to change, she focused on and practiced loving kindness. She became more heart-centered and was finally able to exercise more lovingness toward herself and others.

Once she allowed this shift, Maggie became aware of another destructive behavior she carried. She held on to endless clutter—everything from newspapers to negative thinking. With encouragement, awareness, and intention, she took a deep breath, stepped back, and started cleaning out her closets, her garage, and her barn.

The more healing Maggie experienced in her relationships and the more physical clutter she released from her life, the more she witnessed additional layers of her attachment to control. As she sorted through her closets and cupboards, she began trying to control where the stuff went when she let go of them. "I don't want to give my belongings to this particular charity," she said, "because I hear that if they can't use something they throw it away." When I asked her why she cared, however, she didn't have an answer. She was feeling empty and was trying to fill the empty spaces in the hope she could stop her pain.

We can spend so much time processing and processing our feelings around releasing our belongings that before we know it, another year has gone by and we still have the same old stuff. *We cannot take the stuff with us.* None of this clutter matters. Our bodies are vulnerable and fragile, and we can leave them at any moment. When we die, who is left with the clutter and the stuff?

When I used this analogy with Maggie, she recalled when her mother died. She told me that she and her siblings spent many months trying to clear away the clutter in her mother's home. She said that her parents had never thrown anything away. I asked her if she wanted to do this to her children. Of course her answer was *no,* so I encouraged her to take a leap of faith and bag up what she wanted to release from her life. We talked about her taking her things to a women's shelter, a hospice, or a charitable organization and just let go without worrying how, or if, they will use her discarded stuff.

God will disperse everything to those who have a need. Maybe someone has been praying to receive the very thing we are finally releasing.

As she bravely released her stuff, Maggie's pain was released and she was then free to move further into personal healing.

Attachments

When we are attached to anything, we are disconnected from our Source and our God-self. God is not attached to anything. We can view the world's condition and know that if God was attached, codependent, a fixer, or a caretaker, our world would be a very different place.

God gave everyone free will. That means choice. Unfortunately, many of humankind's choices have created tremendous trauma, destruction, pain, suffering, and death. We need to witness how our negative belief systems, fears, angers, judgments, intolerance, and ignorance have created the world as we know it today. God did not create the challenges. Humankind created them.

To heal and remain connected to the love energy of the Divine intelligence, we must practice detachment. Detachment does not mean we do not love or still care. When we release attachment behavior, we are actually allowing others to have their own journey.

Can you relate to Maggie's behavior? Are you attached to how someone is living his or her life and the choices they make? Are you attached to the decisions your adult children are making? Are you attached to what your spouse eats? Are you attached to what your grandchildren wear? Can you see where your attachments are causing suffering in your life? In your journal, list the ways you are attached to those things in your life that you cannot control and therefore cause you stress, resentment, negativity, and suffering.

Whether emotional, physical, mental, or spiritual,

energy cannot flow where a block exists. Attachment blocks energy. When we feel attached to anything, we usually feel stress and tension somewhere in our body. Where do you feel the tension in your body? Record this in your journal as well. A few years ago, while on a California vacation, I visited one of my brothers. I was already aware of his and his wife's choice to watch the news. (I choose not to watch or read the media's negativity.) But when my brother mentioned they had watched a documentary on world disasters and how the world would end, I immediately became attached to what they were watching and shared my beliefs on how that contributes to fear...blah, blah, blah. I noticed how they physically stepped back; how they looked at me. And I realized right then that I had become attached to their choices. I had gone to fear. I quickly detached and apologized. We are all a work in progress!

One of my students asked me to address the issue of how mothers can possibly detach from their children's choices. Obviously, our parental obligation is to guide and lead our children during their formative years, to become responsible, trustworthy, ethical, integrity-filled human beings. But when our children become adults, we must detach from their choices. We must move into trust that they will make choices for their highest good. It would be foolish for me to tell you this is easy. But it's something we have to do.

Another person's choices regarding their money, their health, or their relationship is *their* business, not ours.

We can demonstrate the God-consciousness by loving unconditionally, supporting, being nonjudgmental, and allowing everyone to make their own choices.

Detachment can seem even more difficult when our loved ones make poor choices, such as drugs, alcohol, or other addictions that take them away from the Truth of who they really are, children of the Light of God.

PAULA

I admire Paula. She was finally able to detach from the choices made by her only child, an adult who has experienced drug addiction for years. She cried, worried, and repeatedly tried to help her twenty-six-year-old son, but he used her, stole from her, and broke her heart over and over. Paula shared with me one of the most difficult decisions that she ever had to make was to detach from her son's choices. After years of anguish, she came to the point where she knew that if she were to really help him and herself, she had to detach. They have very limited contact these days. Paula knows she cannot control her son's choices or behavior, but she can pray for him and hold him in her heart. She knows that someday he will move into the Truth of his Soul's need to grow into his God connection. Someday, Paula prays, her son will accept help and allow healing to take place.

Blessed Detachment Lightens the Soul

Detaching does not mean we do not care and love! It means *we stop fixing.* It means *we release worry, control, and manipulation.* Detaching is one of the most difficult lessons I myself have had to learn.

My son is now a middle-aged man. Every once in a while, he gives me an opportunity to detach all over again. In a mother's heart, our children will always be our children. When my son appears to me in my dreams, he is usually a little boy or a youth. As my beloved son leads his life, I can choose to worry about him; or I can choose to affirm in my mind that he is making the best choices and decisions for his life.

Consciously and subconsciously, we continually create our reality. If we focus our attention on worrying that our loved ones may be making poor choices, we are contributing negative energy to them. That is certainly not my intention with my son. I choose to detach. I say a powerful affirmation and see the Truth of my son as a demonstration of God in form.

But it wasn't easy for me to detach the first time I tried. I kept working at it, and now, after many years of practice, it has become easier. We are much more effective when we are thinking, speaking, and feeling positive energy than when we are wasting time worrying. Worry is a useless emotion. When we worry, we just get more things to worry about. God does not worry. God does not fear. God does not control, or attach.

It is important to hold in our consciousness that God has our back and our children's back. Our family not only has our support, they have the support of the Source of All, whether they know this, or believe it, or not. No matter what our choices, or our family's choices are, we all have the opportunity to connect to the God-self within and maintain that consciousness. The fear-based collective consciousness is filled with doubt and worry. The more we tap into this negative energy, the more difficult life seems. We need to become more and more aware of our negative thinking, STOP it, and use every opportunity to stay in the moment, where God is. The Universe abhors a vacuum. The more worry and negativity you release, the more room you have to receive your good.

Addictions

As I shared previously, whatever we are attached to disconnects us from our Source. Addictions are strong attachments that can numb us and cause separation from God and others. When our emotional or physical body is in great pain, we can be disconnected from our center, which is our Soul.

I need to share a terrifying personal experience of addiction. After my open-heart surgery, I was prescribed oxycodone (Oxycontin). In 2007, I was not aware of the repercussions of taking this lethal drug, which is synthetic heroin created by pharmaceutical companies and prescribed by "dealers with degrees," called medical doctors. It is a very addictive drug.

The dose I was on at the time of my release from the physical rehabilitation facility was twenty milligrams four times a day. This was therapeutically correct for my body at that time, and I was pain-free. Since I did not have an internal medicine doctor at that time, I needed to find one immediately to monitor my post-op medications. I was very concerned about becoming addicted to any medications and needed help to avoid this from happening.

I believe that our physicians need to be members of our personal health care team. They work for us. We have the right to ask questions and to be informed of every decision they make on our behalf. I interviewed three internal medicine physicians. The first one refused my concept of being part of my care team. Saying it was to be *her way, or no way*, she walked out of our meeting.

My second interview was with an internist who agreed with my teamwork concept. After asking her many questions, I decided to become her patient. At that time, however, I was only three weeks out of surgery and on heavy medication. When my new doctor said she wanted to change my oxycodone prescription, I was not clear about her reasoning for doing so. When I asked her why she was changing it to forty milligrams three times a day, she explained that I would not be taking the drug as often as the previous twenty milligrams four times a day. I was unable to think rationally at the time and failed to understand that she had taken me from a total of eighty milligrams a day to one hundred and twenty milligrams a day. This "internist" had increased the narcotic by an additional forty milligrams, with no logical reason or need.

After a month on the new prescription, it ran out. Because oxycodone is a narcotic, there are no automatic refills. I called the doctor's office for a new prescription and was told the doctor was out of town for a week, so there was nothing they could do for me. I explained I had only one pill left and did not want to go through withdrawal. The nurse said not to worry about it and that I would not have withdrawal symptoms.

I took my last pill that night and started the next day without medication. By ten o'clock the next morning I was feeling dizzy and had tunnel vision. Then I began hyperventilating. I experienced full-blown anxiety and felt as though bugs were crawling all over my body. I was in my second floor bedroom, which was large, but I felt like it was closing in around me. I wanted to jump out the window. I called the doctor's office again and described the symptoms to the nurse. I begged for a prescription. She refused to help me. She also denied that I could be in withdrawal and said there was nothing she could do for me.

I could not breathe…I wanted to run outside, but couldn't because I was on oxygen and depended on a walker and the ground was covered with snow. I called my son, Jim, at work, and he immediately came to me. When he asked me how he could help, I told him what was happening and that I wanted to get out of the house as fast as possible. We drove to the doctor's office. While I waited in the car, Jim went in and refused to leave until they gave him my prescription refill order. We got it filled. And within two weeks, I had weaned myself off that terrible drug. Then I called the doctor and fired her butt. I told her how irresponsible, greedy, and negligent I thought she had been.

When I hear about the terrible epidemic of Oxycontin addiction in the United States, which is perpetrated by practitioners in our medical community, I am appalled. I know the truth of addition firsthand. I understand what happens to people taking that drug. I am grateful I was supported by my son, and my God, in helping me escape the addiction and find my way back to health quickly.

Yes, I interviewed a third internist, who is ethical and professional and listens to me and has agreed to be part of my healing team. We have a wonderful patient-doctor relationship.

Own Your *Dukkha*

The Sanskrit word *dukkha* means "suffering." When Siddhartha Gautama, known as the "Enlightened One," the Buddha, spoke about the Four Noble Truths, he said, "The First Noble Truth is the life of *dukkha*." He did not say, "We are here to suffer, or we must suffer." Life brings challenges of mental, emotional, physical, and spiritual pain.

The Second Noble Truth is, "There is a cause of suffering." Suffering is a choice and is caused by attachment to belief systems and things.

The Third Noble Truth is, "There is an end to suffering."

When you see the cause of your suffering, you will have the opportunity to see the end of suffering.

The Fourth Noble Truth is, "There is a path out of suffering." [14] It is up to each of us to find it.

Buddhism is rich in teachings on how to avoid and stay out of *dukkha*. Learn what brings you joy and learn what brings you suffering.

The Unknown Future

The concept of a "future" is an illusion. Time is manmade, not God-made. When we focus our attention on the past, we are mentally recreating perceptions of what was, and when we live in the future of what may be, we are living an illusion and projecting our thoughts into the unknown. Suffering lives in the unknown.

Our experiences of chronos time are really an illusion. Our good, our God, is right here, right now in *kairos* time. If we think something is in the future, we cannot receive it in the now.

Chronos means chronological, or sequential, time. It is manmade. We schedule, plan, use calendars, day planners, watches, clocks, and alarms to remind us of where we are suppose to be sometime in the future. In chronos time, it is about DO-ing, not connecting and BE-ing. In chronos time, we feel separate. We fear we do not have enough time.

Kairos time is Divine time. It is sacred, it is God's time,

---

14 Huston Smith, "Buddhism," in *The World's Religions* (New York: HarperCollins, 1991), pp. 82-99.

it is where we are when we are in meditation and prayer. It is peaceful, healing, and filled with love and light. Kairos time is about BE-ing. This is where we long to BE. In *kairos* time we lose track of time because we are in the continuum of light.

Nothing Changes if Nothing Changes

I recently found a healing-process letter I wrote in my journal sometime after my heart surgery experience. Let me share it here.

> *Dear Heart Attack and Heart Surgery,*
>
> *You came to me uninvited. You were the last experience from which I ever wanted to receive a visit. Thank you for the shock, trauma, fear, physical, and emotional pain!*
>
> *Thank you for the excellent doctors and caretakers I met who showed compassion. Thank you for helping me to discover a deeper level of compassion within myself, as I forgive those hospital and rehab people who were unloving, uncompassionate, and frightening, as I lay helpless for many weeks.*
>
> *Thank you for leading me to ask for help when I have always been so independent. Thank you for teaching me humility.*

Thank you for the endless help and support I received from loved ones. Thank you for helping me learn the difference in "friends" via who left me because I was broken and needy and who stuck by me as I regained my wholeness.

Thank you for the lessons that helped me understand I am meant to be here for now, when I was certain I was going to die.

The change I have experienced since your visit has been immense...but I never want you to visit me again! I promise to remember the good and release the pain.

Namaste.

To heal, we must embrace change. Writing a letter to yourself or the situation can be a very powerful way to move forward. Let your journaling be the process that it is meant to be. There is no right or wrong time to write your letter. I wrote my letter after the traumatic event when I had processed enough, which allowed me to move into gratitude. Sometimes as we are going through a challenging situation, it is helpful to write about our feelings of fear, anger, pain, and our *dukkha*. Our growth and change processes are very individual, very personal. Be kind to yourself.

God Created Change

Are you willing to change? Do you fear change? Do you fight change? When we fear change, we really fear the unknown, the unknown future. If you stay in this moment and do not allow your mind to drift into the what-ifs of future unknowns, change can be swift. It can also be an amazing gift.

It is indeed a waste of valuable energy to resist change. When we are ready and willing to walk away from fear, we are finally embracing change. When we embrace change and allow ourselves to "be in the flow"; surrender what feels unmanageable to God, and breathe, life will not feel so difficult. If you want the good life now then you have to let go of the old life that is holding you back.

After my heart attack and surgery, I experienced constant change, whether I wanted it or not. Looking back, I now embrace the changes that the heart attack and surgery brought to me. Some may say that I had no choice. They are wrong. We always have a choice. I chose to walk through the fire of change; the seasons of change. I chose to live and not to die. Not only did I move through all four seasons of the year during my recovery, but I also realized I had to move into the new seasons of my life. I was seeing changes in my relationships, in abundance, and in my health and receiving them with grace. I was creating my new reality.

Yes, life changes. Days change, the seasons change, the world changes, we change, everyone around us changes. But Spirit's unconditional love never changes. Spirit is always in balance. God is always with us through every season of our life. God takes care of everything, if we will allow it to.

Please, take your journal out again. Now take a deep breath and write what change means to you. What does the thought of change trigger in you? What has been the greatest change in your life? How did you handle it? Where are you today because of it? What do you still want or need to change? Look into your heart. Your Soul knows the answers. Listen to your Soul. Write down what it said and then reread it aloud to your self.

Move into Change

When your negative self-talk dwells on past failures, mistakes, regrets, and disappointments, you may feel deflated, and discouraged, even depressed. You may feel overwhelmed and too fearful to move forward. You're stuck in your story.

When asked her greatest fear, eighty-nine-year-old Maryann replied, "I can never have what I want. I am not good enough. I am not smart enough. Time is running out. I am way too old now to have success. I missed my chance. I blew it. I will never amount to anything."

These were Maryann's beliefs, but that's not how the world saw her. During her life, Maryann raised four children into thriving adults who gave her nine grandchildren and seven great-grandchildren. Maryann was not only a wife for fifty-six years and a mother, but she also created a successful accounting business in her hometown for thirty-five years.

She was deeply respected and loved in her community. She was a member of her church for twenty-five years and served on numerous committees. Even with all her achievements, however, she did not value her own self-worth. She was rooted in regret and her belief that she was not good enough.

GRETA

Take the leap; take a risk. Instead of carrying fear of the unknown, enjoy an adventure. How bad can that be? One of the exciting things about living on this planet is the unexpected magical experience just around the corner. No matter what our age.

I met seventy-nine-year-old Greta at dinner one night while we were both on a Caribbean cruise where I was teaching at a Wellness Conference. We were all sharing our plans for the following day, when the ship would be in port. I asked Greta about the excursion she was planning. "Well, dear," she said, "I'm going zip-lining with my friends tomorrow. I can hardly wait!" She had the biggest smile on her face. She was in joy! Not fear.

When we hold on to our fears like a safety blanket, we are only fooling ourselves. There is nothing safe when fear is involved. When we shut out experiences, people, energy, and opportunities to grow, we are shutting out life itself. We only walk on this planet for a short time (this time around), so why not experience more today than you did yesterday or all the days before?

God's Pocket

One Sunday at our spiritual center, our minister asked us, "How would you feel if you knew you were in God's pocket?" Think about that. How would you feel? When I thought about it, I felt safe and protected. Since then, I have asked many clients that same question. Everyone gives similar answers—"warm, safe, secure, contented, protected." Well, guess what. *You are always in God's pocket.* Your level of awareness of this experience is the key. Allow the feeling of connection to Source to comfort you.

Your power lies in your choices. Every moment, you have choice. You can choose to allow your negative self-talk to demoralize you, or you can immediately choose to think differently. Take a deep breath and turn to God. The Divine Source wants you to be at peace, feel safe, to be in joy, to have success, and to have all the great things in life that you want. If you live in the past or in the future, you will not have enough strength left over to live in the present. All you have is this moment, the Now. Know you have the power to change.

Do not let negative self-talk sabotage you. Do not agree with the negative thoughts that tell you all your faults and limitations. Part of you, your observing self, can observe your self-sabotaging thoughts. Be aware and stand up in the Truth of who you are. Choose to deny the lies. God never lies to you! God only knows the magnificence and the magic of you. You are the child of the Beloved. You always have been, and you always will be, no matter what the outer appearances in your life and no matter what your inner critic or outer critics tell you. It does not matter what you have or have not done in your life, God will never stop loving you. God's love is unconditional and unending. If ego is allowed to live in your thoughts, it will edge God out, and you will not feel the love that is firmly wrapped around you forevermore.

Surrender to Change

"Surrender" is a word that may scare many people. They think that if we surrender, it means we have to give up our personal power. Actually, surrender is a form of releasing control. When we surrender to the Source, we trust the Divine Energy to meet all our needs.

Back in the late 1990s, I was praying to be the best healer I could be. I wanted my skills as an intuitive energy healer and my relationship with the Source to be deeper and stronger. I started to receive messages from the small, still voice of guidance inside me. The messages were clearly about what I needed to change and release in my life so I could receive what I wanted to create. Where did I go? I went to great fear! I kept saying, "No, I can't do that," or, worse yet, I ignored the messages.

I was receiving messages not only from Spirit, but also from many intuitive people, that I would be moving to the mountains in Colorado. Source's messages came through the voices of my son, my friends, and intuitive readers. At that time, I was living in Southern California, five blocks from the ocean, and I ran my counseling practice in a cute little cottage in a counseling center two blocks from the beach. I had no desire to move.

At the same time, I was still praying to be the best healer I could be, I was also ignoring the information, guidance, and direction I was receiving. Have you ever ignored guidance? Of course you have.

Before long, everything in my life started changing. My business declined. My three-year relationship ended. I began to have health challenges. I was still fighting change. The stress became overwhelming because things were changing with or without my conscious approval. You see, I was praying for change and fighting it at the same time. The Universe always says," YES." I was saying *no*. Conflict and confusion within me were the result. Ultimately, when the losses appeared too great, the small voice said, *Now will you move? Will you change your behavior now?*

When I was three days from being evicted from my home, I finally surrendered. It's okay to yell at God. God does not care. So I yelled, "Fine! If you want me on the street, I'll live on the street! You want me to change, I'll change. Whatever you want—fine! I'll do it! I surrender! I cannot do this anymore."

This was the biggest and most profound surrender of my life. Starting that evening, everything changed.

I kept my promise. So did Spirit. I did not end up on the street. My business increased again, and my health improved. I set my Colorado move date for six months later, and I did not need to postpone it. Source provided me with full abundance. I made enough money to not only hire movers and make the interstate move, but also to pay off all my debts and take two months off to relocate, acclimate, create a website, and restructure my private practice in a beautiful small town in Colorado.

In late October, 2000, my son drove me from California to Colorado, pulling my car and carrying all my belongings in a rental truck. Driving in the rain through the mountains near the Continental Divide, Jim and I gasped as we both saw an awesome sight. We drove through the end of a rainbow in the middle of the highway in front of us. We always hear about the "pot of gold at the end of the rainbow," but how many people actually have the opportunity to spend a moment in time, a split-second, in the energy of such a phenomenon? It was magical. I saw it as a sign that I had made the right decision, and I have never regretted my move. I have been richly rewarded for following Source's guidance. You see, when we surrender and live in alignment with our Source, God always makes the crooked path straight and brings us rainbows.

The two biggest lessons I learned were (1) to trust God and (2) that I always have choice. In addition, I learned to be aware of what I ask for. In order for my prayer to be answered, for me to be the best healer I could be, I had to make the changes Spirit directed me to. That was where the answers to the prayer were. *A piece of ordinary coal, under tremendous pressure, becomes a rare diamond.*

I physically moved. I moved emotionally and mentally, too, and I spiritually moved into integrity and alignment with the Universal Laws. I got more than I prayed for when

I asked to be the best healer I could be. Not only did my skill level increase when I cleaned out my mental closets, but abundance, happiness, and good came to me in many ways. I learned, albeit the hard way, to do what my Soul and my God support me to do. The Buddhist teaching is that *nothing remains without change.*

A Releasing Process

This world is so full of fear that sometimes we just don't know where our fears came from. Surely the beginning of our fear started at home when we were children. Along our journey to where we are today, we have met many people who have influenced our lives in positive and negative ways. We do not always remember who influenced us, or how they did it, and we might wonder where we picked up so much negativity.

Take out your journal and write the fears you have been carrying that do not feel like they belong to you. These fears may be fears of risk-taking, change, lack, abandonment, loss, disease, even death. Whose fears are you carrying? Take your time and write everything that comes to you.

Guided Meditation #4

(Consider recording the following meditation.)

Close your eyes, take a deep breath, and envision the people who knowingly and unknowingly demonstrated their fears. See them standing in front of you. You subconsciously took their fears on as your own. Hand them the list of fears that you have been carrying for them. Imagine that they are receptive, that they take responsibility for their own fears. (This may feel like a stretch if you have never seen them take responsibility for anything before. It's all right. This is your fantasy, your release, so you can "direct" it any way you want it to go.)

Watch as they reach out and take the list in their hands. They're taking back everything they said to you, everything you accepted as your truth, not theirs. See them walk away with the list of fears. Allow yourself to take another deep breath as you release the hold you had on that list and the hold these people had on you. Take as long as you need. When you are ready to open your eyes, do so. Take another deep breath.

It is now time to tear the old list to shreds and bury or burn the shredded paper. Whatever way you choose to release this old energy is great. Just do it!

Affirmational Prayer

Take a deep breath and close your eyes. Allow the energy of the Universe to enter your crown chakra, which is at the top of your head. Imagine a golden light moving down through your entire body. As you exhale, imagine any unwanted blocks, attachments, and fears being released through your fingertips or the bottoms of your feet. Breathe in the light of love and exhale the darkness of fear and blocks as you say this affirmation aloud to yourself and your Source.

God's abundance of unconditional love is right here in this moment. It is wrapped around me and supports me at all times. Every breath I take is God in form. As God works through me and as me, I am thankful for the knowing that I am the co-creator of my life.

I am aware that my words are demonstrated in my life as my reality. I choose to release all fears and attachments that hold me in negative thoughts.

I trust that my loved ones make decisions that fully benefit their lives. I accept the Divine love and abundance in my own life and in theirs as I trust that my loved ones are fully happy, healthy, and magnificently abundant in all areas of their lives.

I trust and know God's full support for all of us on our path. With this knowing, I release fear, control, and attachment. I surrender it into Source's care.

I give great thanksgiving as I release this affirmation into the Universal Law for complete manifestation in the now.

And so it is, Amen.

Practice this process on a daily basis until you feel completely relaxed and peaceful. Breathe. Release and let go. Choose to think differently.

~ Part 2 ~

Discover Your Soul's Desire

OUR SOUL'S DESIRE

Our Soul is part of the huge Universal Soul. The Universal Soul wants our human Soul to know of its existence, to be aware of the brilliant Light that it is. Our Soul chose this human experience to grow and heal by releasing all fears and moving into forgiveness for our own choices and the choices others make.

Having a Soul is universal. Everyone has one. The difference in Souls is one's level of consciousness of its existence. When you want to discover your Soul's purpose, ask yourself first if you have discovered your Soul. Do you feel it? Have you learned the Truth of your Soul? Who is it? Your Soul is not separate from you. *It is you.* What it is not, is your negative ego-self.

As our Soul heals and moves into a higher vibration, it affects the human community of Souls, our human race consciousness. The level of consciousness in which we live directly influences the collective consciousness of every Soul on this planet. We can tip the scale, as it were, to reach the highest level of God/Soul consciousness that has ever moved upon this earth. Our Soul desires to serve all of life through mindfulness, thoughtfulness, compassion, understanding, humility, and full-hearted love. Through this elevated Soul Consciousness, peace will prevail.

Where there is a display of negativity in any form in or upon this planet, we must first identify how it affects us. To move out of the fear, use your STOP light to keep the ego from rising, then quickly move into Soul consciousness. Send light to the situation. Send light to the Souls in conflict. Be that which is the God mentality. Embody the Wiccan Rede, which is to *Do No Harm*.[15]

When I leave this life, I want my Soul to be fully complete in its awareness. I want my light to shine brightly with God's Light.

Living in Passion and on Purpose

What is your passion? Are you practicing your purpose? Many people have come to me and asked, "What are my passion and my purpose in this lifetime?" But that's not for me to answer. The only person who can answer that question is you.

What is your personal passion in life? What do you love to do? What makes your heart sing? If your ego weren't telling you that you can't do what you really love to do, what would you choose to do?

---

15   John J. Coughlin, *Ethics and the Craft: The History, Evolution, and Practice of Wiccan Ethics* (New York, Waning Moon Publications, 2009). See http://www.waningmoon.com/ethics/

Your contract, or purpose, is right in front of you. It has always been in your heart. Maybe someone else is telling you that what you're dreaming of doing or being is not okay. Or, that you will never be able to make money by living your dream because it's not a "real job." It's important to know they are speaking from their own limitations, their own fears. Do not let their fears become your fears. Trust yourself and keep your heart's desire.

From the day I started grade school, I thought it would be fun to be a teacher. Each day, after school I gathered all my little friends together, set them down in front of me, stood at a toy chalkboard, and played schoolteacher. You can only imagine the looks on their faces. My playmates' eyes glazed over. I was expecting them to play school with me when we had just left school. On top of that, I had to be the teacher. Although I did not grow up with the intention of making a living as a teacher, today I create classes and teach people from all over the world. I also write articles, poetry, lyrics, and books. My Soul has cried out to be creative for as long as I can remember.

Your Soul has likewise cried out to express itself. Have you been paying attention? If not, you may feel like you have a big hole in your chest or stomach. You may not feel complete. That's because your Soul is trying to get your attention. Now is the time to pay attention. Now is the time to move through your fears. Imagine what you would be doing if you had no fear regarding time, location, money, or what other people think. What do you feel excited about? Do not be afraid to admit what that may be. Surprise yourself.

I don't know your pain and how or if you struggle, but I have yet to meet anyone who has not had their share of life's challenges. You may say your life has been a nightmare and no one with the awful childhood you had could expect to have a good life now. *Well*, I reply, *you can keep sitting there with your pain and torment... or you can get up, suit up, and show up!* And when you do, your life will change. You can live your drama... or you can live your dream. If you think someone else will carry you across the finish line, you are truly mistaken. It is your responsibility to be your own greatest supporter.

The Gospel According to John tells us that Jesus approaches a man in Jerusalem who has been crippled for thirty-eight years and had been lying around feeling sorry for himself and waiting for a miracle. As this man held on to his despair and old resentments and wounds, he was not moving into forgiveness, which only added to his disorder. Jesus asked him, "Do you want to be made well?" Jesus was really asking what this man's intention was for his life. Did he just want to continue lying around feeling sorry for himself? Or did he want something better? The man tried to make excuses for his lack of change by blaming others for the circumstances of his life, but Jesus did not buy into his self-pity. He looked at the man and said, "If you really want to get well and want to make a better life for yourself, you will have to pick up your belongings and get on your way." When the man followed Jesus' instruction, he was "miraculously" healed. [16]

Like the man in the Bible, we can just lie around feeling sorry for ourselves or we can get up and declare our desire to change. Fear of not "doing it right" is a waste of time and energy. It truly is not important what others think or what others have told you or how others have treated you. Make a decision today to get up, pick up your belongings, and show up for your life. Your decisions effect the entire world.

Take a risk. Enter a class, a training program, or a workshop in what you love or what you feel called to do in your life. Have you always wanted to dance? Does your Soul want to sing? Do you want to create something? Do you want to teach? Do you want to minister to others? Every one of us has our own unique talent and depth of Divine energy under the talent.

Let your light shine and your Soul demonstrate itself through living and doing what you came here to do and how you came to serve humanity. Every single God-given profession on this planet serves humanity in some way. The desire to live on purpose was placed in your heart and inner knowing before you were born. Go to God, go to guidance, go to silence, and find your treasure. It rests in your Soul. Who knows—you may have been brought to this time and place in history to make a difference. When it is shown to you, just shout, "Yes!"

---

16   John 5:1-9, *Holy Bible, from the Ancient Eastern Manuscripts,* translated by George M. Lamsa (A.J. Holman, 1933-1968).

Soul-Discovery Journey

Know that all the processes, journaling, meditations, prayers, and releases you have been led through, and will further experience in this book, are leading you to Soul-discovery. Again, I suggest you record the following journey script for your ease in participating more fully.

Guided Meditation #5

Make yourself comfortable and take a deep breath. Fully accept the relaxing energy that is flowing through your crown chakra at the top of your head and down through your physical body. This warm golden light from the Universe releases all tension in your head...neck...shoulders. Allow yourself to become aware that the healing energy flows down both arms, and all of your stress flows right out through your fingertips.

Another deep breath of cleansing air fills your lungs and assists every organ and system in your body to relax. Peaceful, warm energy flows down your spine and around your lower back, your hips, and down through your legs. Allow the release of tension and tightness to exit through the bottoms of your feet.

Now focus your attention on the center of your forehead, between and a little above your brows. This is the sixth chakra, the third eye. This is the seat of awareness. With your inner eye, look up and into this space. Here you find a source of light. It may be any lovely color that comes to you. It's okay if you do not see it. You may hear its tone, or you may feel its vibration. In any case, you know it is there. *It has always been there.*

As you move fully into awareness of this magnificent energy, allow yourself to simultaneously see, hear, and feel your connection to your heart center, your fourth chakra. This connection between your inner eye and your heart center represents the love connection you have with the Universal One. This is where your Soul "lives." It lives in the seat of Love...in the center of Love...in the space of All-Knowing. This IS the Truth of you.

We live in this physical form on this planet and at this time, for a specific reason. Experience the deep stillness within you. Maintain awareness that you are part of a deep...deep...deep...connection. This energy of the One that we call by many names lives within us and *AS US.*

From this space and with your full awareness of connection, allow yourself to receive a message from your Soul now. 1, 2, 3...breathe. You may receive one word or many. There is no right or wrong. Be still within this sacred place for as long as you are comfortable and experience your deep connection to your Soul. Take your time.

When you are ready to come back into full awareness of your physical body, take another deep breath with the intention of surfacing. Stretch and move, to fully embrace your physical experience again.

Know you can visit this deep level of awareness in your third eye (sixth chakra) and heart center (fourth chakra) anytime you wish. Become familiar and comfortable with connecting to your Soul essence. Your Soul knows and remembers every one of your lifetimes and is fully aware of your purpose here and every step on your journey. It has come here again to learn and grow.

Be in Service

When we open our hearts to help others, we are in service. We may see an elderly woman sitting in her wheelchair, having trouble as she tries to button her sweater. Why not ask her if she would like some help? What if you see someone struggling with heavy bags of groceries as they are walking to their front door? Do you ignore them and hope they don't see you, or will you offer your help? Of course, you *can*, but *will you*? When was the last time you allowed another driver to pull in front of you without getting upset? Offering such small kindnesses is serving others. We can be stuck in thinking we have to do something huge to qualify as service to others, but the small things are just as useful in the world. Consider being loving, kind, conscious, nonjudgmental, and aware of another's needs. Be unafraid to connect with another human being. Offer your help to a person in need. Remember that service to others is not about you.

Your purpose is right in front of you. Just reach out and grab it. Trust that the Universal energies have guided you to this moment and will continue to guide you. Pay attention. In my experience, all the different occupations, trainings, and endeavors I went through in corporate America served as a foundation to the business I have today. I didn't know this back then, but I was being groomed to have my own business. I attempted several self-employment opportunities through the years, and each of those experiences also helped me. They were practice for what I do now. Trainings in my field of interest were brought to me as I needed them. Each one of my learning opportunities has served me well.

We don't always know what Source has in store for us. When we say *yes* and open ourselves to the possibilities that are brought to us in a variety of ways, we are on the journey of discovering our true purpose on the planet.

Accept Your Creativity

What is creativity? According to Webster's[17] it means "ability to produce something new through imaginative skill, whether a new solution to a problem, a new method or device, or a new artistic object or form. The term generally refers to a richness of ideas and originality of thinking."

Everyone is creative, either knowingly or unknowingly. Creativity is a gift we all receive. It's a gift that enriches our lives and the lives of others. Creativity enriches our Soul. Our gifts are meant to be shared. The world can only thrive if we can grow and share our talents, our creativity, and our individuality. When we recognize our purpose and make ourselves of service to others, we are helping to change the world into a more loving and peaceful place. Dance with great authenticity in who you are and what you bring to the world.

---

17   *Merriam-Webster's Dictionary*, 2005.

BOBBIE

Bobbie was born to be a singer. She sang her heart out when she was a child. It made her happy and filled with joy to share her voice and write her songs. But her mother told her she sounded like a toad. Unfortunately, Bobbie believed her and shut her voice down...along with her creativity. As she grew into an adult, however, she began to allow herself to sing in the car and in the shower. But she sang only to herself, never where anyone could hear her.

Bobbie's Soul contract to serve through her creative voice was trying to resurface. But one relationship partner after another challenged her by saying *no* to her dreams, based on their fears. She no longer was hearing that she had a bad voice; now she was being told her voice was beautiful but that she should not think she could ever make a living by singing. Bobbie's first husband said he didn't want her to be unavailable to him. He told her to put her dreams aside, and once again she denied her Soul's desire.

As Bobbie shared her relationship history with me, she blamed everyone else for her not living her dream of singing. It was no wonder she brought physical issues of heart pains and stomach pains to our session to be healed.

Spirit worked through me to heal Bobbie's physical condition. Spirit also showed me what needed to be cleared on the emotional level. Bobbie was carrying years and years of anger at giving up her heart's passion, and she could no longer "stomach" her choice to listen to others and not herself.

This may sound simple. It is simple. What we think is what we create. Bobbie thought she had no right to sing, write songs, or live her passion. For a long time, she thought her mother's criticisms were true. Today, she is working on releasing the fears of others that she integrated into her own fears. She has had to identify whose fears are whose. She is no longer married to the man who tried to quash her dreams of singing. She has chosen to take singing lessons to strengthen her voice. Today she is choosing to enjoy and share her talents. Today Bobbie is feeling better about herself.

We only have today. This very day needs to be filled with self-love and self-commitment. How are you honoring yourself? Are you allowing yourself to hear the small, all-knowing voice of Spirit and letting it guide you to what you love? How can you be all you can be? Do you allow creativity to move through you? Do you allow yourself to change and move into the unknown? Or do you move into fear?

A Choice to Serve

What are you bringing into your life and into the lives of others? Are you displaying negative energy and thoughts by perpetrating your own fearful behavior? Or are you a catalyst for good? How do you serve others? How do you make a difference in your community?

By serving a group of elders who live in a residential memory-care facility for patients with Dementia and Alzheimer disease in my community, I have received a great deal of inspiration. My heart is filled with joy when I am assisting these loving beings by spending time with them and listening to their fears. One of the often-shared fears is of being alone. Some elders who cannot remember visits just the day before or the passing of loved ones decades ago, ask for their family members. Many of these beautiful Souls wait endlessly for visits. These memory-challenged residents are very childlike. I learned early on that I do not have to be anything but pure love for them. I bring kindness, attention, hugs, and lots of love, and their smiles and gratitude fill my heart in return. This simple activity of being in a heartfelt place, being in the moment, heals my heart and theirs. And sometimes I witness them setting their fears aside as they laugh, play, sing, and dance.

One of these delightful Souls always holds a positive attitude. Although she is hunched over with osteoporosis, uses a walker, and is in obvious pain—she always answers, "Nothing but the best!" when I ask how her day is going,

These weekly visits with my elderly friends take me outside my personal challenges. I forget about everything but the loving elders with whom I am spending time. I see and feel God as I look into their aging, watery eyes. I remind them that God is with them at all times and no matter what appearances may be, *they are loved and not alone.*

Deserving to Receive

It gives God great pleasure to supply us with all our good. Are you able to receive your good? Receiving is not only a gift to the receiver, but it's also a gift to the person giving.

I think most people feel good about giving to others, but when it comes to receiving graciously, there's a challenge. If this sounds familiar to you, ask yourself, "What created my thought pattern?" Write the answer(s) in your journal. Maybe you were taught by your family or your religion that you should not ask for things. Maybe you were taught the false belief that it is "more blessed to give than to receive." I want to stand up and proclaim that *it is blessed to receive!* What is wrong with receiving? God is not the one who tells us we should not receive. God wants you to have everything and anything you can conceive of.

God gives us everything we believe in and as much as we think we are worth. God's bounty is ours to receive. We are the beloved children of the Source. We are heirs to the throne. But if this is so, then why can we not receive all that the kingdom has to offer?

When we really remember and understand that God is the source of our supply, support, and our substance, our abundance will change for the better. When you change your thinking to *God is my employer, and I am paid well,* your prosperity will grow. If you believe that whoever writes your paycheck is only a go-between from God to you and that God provides the abundance, you will create a new prosperity reality.

Many years ago, I lived in a belief of lack of abundance. Every Sunday evening, I checked my weekly calendar and counted the number of sessions I had booked for the upcoming week. Then I calculated how much money that represented as income. If a client canceled an appointment,

I immediately fell into fear. But fear creates more fear and more stress. I was definitely feeling a lot of stress!

Then I learned that my clients are not in charge of, or responsible for, my income. God is! As I keep myself in gratitude and alignment with the Source, my abundance continually increases. Another important lesson for me was remembering that when a client changed their appointment and a space opened up, there was another client who needed that time slot more than the person who canceled.

God's Abundance

Take a moment to reflect on how your primary caretakers, your family, and other members of your Soul group demonstrate their relationship with finances and personal power.

Money is simply energy that creates a sense of freedom, choice, security, and power. If money is misused, as when any energy is misused, it creates negativity, fear, and challenges instead.

Our abundance is God-given. It comes from the Source. It may appear that it comes from your employer, clients, customers, the government, a charity, a company, an inheritance, your parents, or your spouse.... But it does not. *They are the vehicles.* Abundance moves via these vehicles from God to you.

When we live with the knowing that God is the Source of our supply, substance, and support, we are in alignment with our abundance. When we know and feel that God moves through us and as us, we can then accept the concept that we are one with our Source of abundance. Being in the flow and the awareness of our greatness and ability to be a source of co-creatorship with God allows us to experience more good in our lives.

Our thoughts create our reality. We receive what we already know we have. If we feel we have struggle, we will have more struggle. If we think and feel we are worthy of more good, more of the blessings are available to us. As heirs to the universal throne, we will indeed receive more good in our lives. Almost every religious and spiritual teaching has the message that our life is shaped by our mind and we become what we think. Our Soul longs to be free of the egoic fears and free to fly toward Divine Truth.

Your God is your good. Your GOOD shows itself to you in the abundance of good health, financial security, and healthy and happy relationships. Open yourself first to your God, then to your Good, and witness what happens. Claim Good into your life right here, right now. Accept Good as your experience of God's Truth of absolute abundance in all good things.

Fear of Failure and Success

It is possible to fear both failure and success at the same time. What we fear, we draw to ourselves. Therefore it follows that if we fear failure, we will create failure through inertia, indecisiveness, inactivity, procrastination, and self-sabotage. We can actually be successful at creating our own failure.

Failure is an illusion and a judgment held in our society. The perception of failure is the opportunity to do something different the next time. Seeing the opportunity as an experience to learn what didn't work shows us what we need to change. God does not consider us or our choices as failures. Ego criticizes, judges, and labels circumstances as failures. Nothing is good or bad in God's awareness. *It just is.*

It is useless to blame others for our failures. We create our own reality. Our choices are demonstrated in what we experience. We are always in choice, and we are much more powerful than we think we are.

It's time to identify with abundance and success as your true nature.

Limited Thinking

This next story illustrates the deep-rooted belief system of poverty consciousness that is held by the collective "church" community. Their common belief is that only 20 percent of the congregation volunteers do 100 percent of the work. If you ask almost any minister or spiritual leader in your community, they will validate this belief.

Many years ago, I attended a "visioning" gathering at a spiritual center. In case you're unfamiliar with visioning, it is a process where the attendees sit in silence and connect to Source to receive direction around a certain issue. The visioning I attended was for the purpose of direction for the growth and development of the spiritual center. After the visioning process was complete, each attendee had an opportunity to share what information Spirit provided to them.

I was given a very clear message for our group *to change their old belief from 20/80 to 80/20—or, better yet—100 percent volunteer participation by 100 percent of the center's population.* We can never ask for too much. As we believe, so we will receive.

The group leader gave me a look of disbelief. Then they said, "Well, maybe we should work on getting to 40 percent first, and when we reach that, we can work on getting to 60 percent...and so forth." I was taken aback. The comment demonstrated lack of belief in the possibility of big change and God's abundance.

If we don't change our thinking, nothing in our experience can change.

When I went home that evening after that visioning circle and the leader's reaction to my vision, I went into meditation, asking the Source to help me with my challenge of not being heard by this community.

I received the following message through clairaudience:[18]

Don't stop BE-ing in Truth, the Truth of the I AM. You know the Truth of what you have brought forth to this community. Do not give up. Be a demonstration

---

18   *Merriam-Webster's Dictionary*, 2005: "The power or faculty of hearing something not present to the ear but regarded as having objective reality."

of how it works to be in Christ consciousness. In your work, you ask for a healing, you believe it, and it is done. Others have the opportunity to see this. Bring this Truth to them. You are a minister of the Truth, of healing, and manifestation. You administer the message every day. You are free of doubt. You are an example. Do not pull away in fear of what others think. Stay present in your connection to the Universal Law. You are being guided. As you believe so shall you receive. If you want to help this community to survive and grow, you will be shown how. You have been given the message for this group. Now, go forward and present this opportunity to the leader without attachment to the outcome. See the Truth, bring Truth forward, and trust others will see the Truth. It is not for you to change them. It is for you to present the Truth as given. Your will is my will. As you believe, It is so.

It does not matter what the organism is. If we, as co-creators of the world, do not believe something can heal 100 percent, it won't. When I co-create with Source to bring about an emotional or physical healing for a client, I don't claim a 40 percent healing, I claim a 100 percent healing, and that's what shows up.

There are multiple healing techniques available to us today. Not one is better than another, when they are God-given. The key is the Truth, knowing, and trust of God's healing. Always remember that God is the healer and It does not do sloppy work.

We are co-creators with the Source. God does not say

you can only heal in small increments. That's the negative ego talking. Does it frighten you to think big? Does it frighten you to imagine—and believe—that you can have 100 percent health, 100 percent prosperity, and 100 percent happiness in your life? If you go to disbelief, doubt, fear of failure, and rejection of this possibility, you will never reach your dream.

Pay attention to your limited thinking. We are works in process, yes, but that doesn't mean we aren't allowed to keep the dream, the light at the end of the tunnel, in our thoughts, feelings, visions, and the words we speak. It is our duty. We owe it to ourselves. What is worse—staying in limitation and want, or believing and receiving our dreams?

Near where I live is a very large spiritual center, the Mile Hi Church of Religious Science[19], which does not demonstrate these fears. It has massive attendance and membership. I cannot speak for its 20/80 percent volunteer participation philosophy, although by the looks of its prosperity and community involvement, I would say they have healed that wound.

Money Consciousness

Our country has gone through many economical crises and recovered many times. It will recover again. When the media carry fear-based messages to the population, they do a strong disservice to humanity. No matter what the outer

---

19   Mile Hi Church, Science of Mind and Spirit, Lakewood, Colorado, http://www.milehichurch.org/

appearances of lack, loss, or poverty may be, do not go to fear.

This is a perfect time to explore the belief systems you were taught as a child regarding money. Open your journal and begin writing. As you write, you will learn a lot about yourself regarding your money fears. Look at the belief systems that were carried in your family. What family stories about money did you internalize and integrate into your life? Many people say that their families thought it was taboo to discuss financial information. *But money is energy.* When we fear discussing it, sharing it, or using it, we block the energy flow that lets us receive it. Take another moment to complete your list of the lessons that were demonstrated to you about money issues within your family circle.

Many of us are children or grandchildren of Depression Era families. Because of what was experienced in their lives during those trying times, our parents and grandparents, and maybe our great grandparents, often lived in fear of poverty, lack, and the what-ifs of the future. These emotional genetics have affected our abundance consciousness as well. If we don't change our feelings, along with the words we speak and thoughts we think about money, our future generations will continue to hold the same fear-based cycle of recession and poverty consciousness.

Representatives of Habitat for Humanity came to our spiritual center to present an opportunity for our members to train as coaches for families experiencing homelessness as they are learning to gain, or regain, stability. The representatives spoke of generational poverty and situational poverty. I was delighted when these issues were addressed. There definitely is a difference between the two concepts.

Generational poverty is when two or more generations have lived in poverty and hold the belief systems and behaviors of lack. Pretty much everyone living in this country has been affected generationally by the Great Depression of 1929 as well as subsequent recessions, up to and including the Great Recession of 2008. Situational poverty, on the other hand, is less historical. It is created by a sudden job loss, divorce, or medical problem. Situational poverty is typically temporary and when people get back on their feet, things can get back to normal. In both generational and situational poverty, education and the opportunity to change are crucial elements of climbing out of the poverty experience.

LENNY

Born in 1925, Lenny grew up to be a Depression Era child who carries fears of lack and loss. Growing up, she learned how to preserve food that her family either grew or had access to in large quantities. It was very nutritious, organic food, and they were truly blessed. As she grew and began raising her own family, she also canned and preserved foods for later use. This is a beautiful activity.

Lenny's first realization that she might have a poverty consciousness came when she was in her sixties, divorced, and living alone, yet her refrigerator was so packed with food that when she opened the door she could not get another thing into it. Her freezer was equally stuffed, with no room for more. She also had a full-size freezer in her garage that contained enough frozen food to supply the local grocery store. She continued to make jams and jellies, can vegetables, and store many other wonderful goods, which she always shared with friends and family when they visited. Because her cupboards where overflowing, she stored the newly canned goods in boxes in her guest room.

Lenny does not have an eating problem, but her behavior regarding food clearly demonstrates her food issues from those hard times. Now eighty-five years old, she does not cook anymore, but she still stockpiles and hoards food…"just in case." Her behavior exemplifies the fear of not having enough, not trusting that there is enough in the world, and not believing that *there is more where that came from*. But when everything you need is in front of you, the appearance of lack may be your experience when you are looking through eyes of scarcity.

Hoarders never feel complete enough, full enough, or satisfied enough. No matter how full their larders are or how full their bank accounts are, they never feel that they have enough. I believe this is because they do not feel they are good enough or deserving enough. *Poverty issues are spiritual issues.* Lack of abundance consciousness begins with a lack of God consciousness and how the Law of Attraction and the Law of Circulation work. Simply said, the law of attraction demonstrates itself through *what we think, believe, say, and feel, is what we draw to us.* The law of circulation is *what energy you put out into the world is what comes back to you*

The Universe continually provides all that we need when we need it, no matter what the outer appearances may be. When we move into trust, however, knowing that we live in an abundant Universe and God provides our good, we can be in peace, knowing our success is here now, waiting for us to receive it. There is not a spot where God is not.

Poverty Consciousness

Countries and cultures have collective belief systems. The world has its collective belief system. We see greed, fear, lack, and poverty all around us and it is ingrained in the American culture, even though most of the world sees America as the land of wealth, milk, and honey. The current economic climate is no surprise. The cosmos is now shifting into balance and as it does so, a great darkness will always surface for potential healing.

Why do so many people have so little money? Why do some people attract money and then lose it all? Why do people sabotage themselves when it comes to abundance while others are able to manifest, enjoy, and grow their financial worth? Underlying all these questions are self-esteem issues and beliefs regarding deserving or not deserving prosperity. Thought creates form. If we truly feel, know, and trust down to our deepest subconscious level that we deserve abundance, we will manifest abundance.

The Universe always hears our messages loud and clear. We may be sending messages that we do not want to send by thinking and speaking negativity. When we experience an inner prosperity conflict, we will experience outer lack. This sabotage is driven by ego. Remember, ego projects fear, distrust, and disbelief into our subconscious and therefore into our world. Ego will keep us in turmoil remembering the past financial challenges or projecting the future possibilities of failing. What a waste of our energy this is! When we focus on pennies, we miss God's treasure chest.

Our subconscious believes everything it is told. The subconscious mind does not criticize, but ego does. If you are hearing negative thoughts about yourself, your lack of abundance, your lack of abilities, your lack of talent, your worthlessness, or whatever negativity runs through your mind, please know that this is NOT God talking to you. All negative thoughts come from a place of untruth.

Remember to use the STOP light you were taught in the beginning of this book. Do not let the inner critical thinking waste your time and ruin your life. It truly does not matter how we were raised. Although the experiences of our early years may have been difficult and terrifying at best, we can choose to forgive and move into the reality of this moment. Holding on to the negative words we were given by others diminishes us. In your imagination, hand the negative words back, along with loving forgiveness, to the wounded Soul that gave them to you. Surrender the painful memories and anger to the Source. Forgive yourself for living in negativity. Let go. Breathe!

Risk-Taking

Source brings us opportunities to change, grow, and move into territories we have not walked before. If I have learned anything in this life, it is that as one door closes and the next door opens, Source always brings more good. I have experienced more joy and abundance since I learned to take risks than ever before in my life.

Don't waste your life living in fear. The dark thinking drains your energy and tells you lies. It tells you that you cannot do what you want to do. It tells you that you cannot be what you want to be. If you listen to the negative thoughts that live in the dark side of your mind, your life will become darker and darker. Soon depression and lack of self-worth can set in. Do not allow this negative self-talk to tell you that you are stuck where you are and don't deserve and cannot have better. Know the shift is here now. Step into it.

You deserve to have all your dreams come true. Dream BIG. God is bigger than any dream you can imagine. If other people tell you that you cannot do what you want to do, walk away. Do not let anyone hold you back from being your true self, from fulfilling your dreams, or from knowing and living your Soul's purpose.

Thou Shall Not Steal

We know that fear-based individuals steal from others. But this is not God's behavior. Stealing is not only taking material things from someone else or from a group or corporate entity; it's also attempting to hold another individual down emotionally. It's stealing another person's joy, which is just as negative and cruel as theft or burglary. If you've been dealing with lack and negative thinking in your life, have you felt envy or jealousy because a friend or family member has moved ahead financially, socially, or academically? Do you resent it when someone you know finds love, moves into health, or is blessed in everything they do? As you wish limitation on others, you are energetically stealing their good from them. Remember the law of circulation…if you wish limitation on others, you will experience limitation in your own life.

Of course negative thinking manifests in the world. No one is surprised that negativity exists. However, it is time for us all to focus on change. Allow yourself to know that you, too, can focus on thinking differently and have more blessings in your life than you can ever imagine. To do so, you need to release your beliefs in scarcity, limitation, and resentment.

Journal your thoughts and feelings that surface as you think about the following questions. Who and what are you jealous or envious of? Do you wish negativity on another person? Do you steal another person's light by gossiping?

Greed

Greed is not about money. Greed is when you take more than you give.

–Iyanla Vanzant [20]

Guilt about Abundance

Do you feel guilty because you make more money than other members of your family of origin? Guilt is a useless emotion. You are not taking abundance away from anyone else by being abundant. You can forego all your abundance and empty your bank accounts, but it will not ease the suffering of the have-nots. Do not allow anyone else to project his or her pain and fears onto your life. Everyone else has just as many opportunities for success and abundance as you do, no matter what their "story" is. No one is better than another. God does not show preferences. God does not give more to one person than another. God gives according to your thinking, your feelings, and the words you speak.

Claim your good. Claim your abundance. Claim your prosperity. God is good and good is God. They are one and the same. God is abundant. God is prosperous. We are all equally deserving in the eyes of God.

You are responsible for your own belief in abundance. You are in charge of your thoughts. It is important to be a responsible role model for your children and other family

---

20   Iyanla Vanzant, host of *Fix My Life*, on Oprah Winfrey Network, 2013.

members. You are not here to fix them. You are here to change yourself into being all you can be.

Competition

There is more than enough money to go around. There are more than enough opportunities, customers, clients, abundance for everyone. Competition is only a fear-based perception.

If you operate from a healthy competitive belief system, you will rejoice when others in the same line of business as you join your community. You will welcome the opportunity to network and work together to bring choice and abundance to all concerned. You will feel gratitude when others are happy and fulfilled.

No matter what your business is, do not concern yourself with the concept of competition being a threat. Do not allow yourself to buy into the negative fear-based belief system. Fear of competition is not a useful motivator. Remember what we put our attention on is what we get more of.

MARGO

Many years ago, Margo owned a bakery in a small Midwestern town. She had owned and operated it successfully for twenty years, but she often became angry because similar businesses opened in the newer parts of town. She was afraid they would take business away from her. No matter how many times she was reassured that these so-called competitors were not a threat, she still felt afraid of losing business. Her lack of self-esteem and fear kept her from being happy.

We are all unique. People may seem to be in the same field of work we're in, but everyone brings something different to the table. What we have to offer is needed and wanted by someone. And here we are, right where we are meant to be.

If we see that our real competition is within ourselves, we can strive every day to do and be better in our own lives and not concern ourselves with what others are doing.

Are You Lucky?

What is luck? The dictionary's definition of luck is "accidental fortune, good or bad; fate; chance." I feel the need to disagree. "Accidents" by this definition indicate we have no choice or responsibility for the results. Remember the old saying, *Send someone out to find a quarter on the sidewalk, and, by gosh they will find a quarter on the sidewalk*? It's another example of the truism that what we focus on is what we create. We become what we believe. If you believe you are unlucky, you will indeed be unlucky. But if you believe you are lucky, you will feel lucky.

Make a choice to *feel lucky, believe that you're lucky*, and *receive your luck*. We do not have to be told that we were born under a lucky star or born with Jupiter (the so-called lucky planet) as our ruling planet to feel a Divine flow with All That Is.

Many think luck is when it looks like things are going their way, but this is really another demonstration of belief systems—what we think is what we get. If we determine, decide, own, claim, and proclaim our bounty of luck, so it is. The Universe always says, "Yes." Does luck really exist? If in your heart you believe it does and you believe you deserve it, then it will exist in your life.

I don't believe in bad luck. It's all about your perception. If you say you have bad luck, you do. The Universe says *yes* to negative thinking as fast as it says *yes* to positive thinking. See how powerful you are?

Ordinary Miracles

What is a miracle? The dictionary says a miracle is "a wonder; a phenomenon, a supernatural happening." I say that a miracle is the evidence of living in alignment with our God. Every day, we get to choose to stay connected to God and witness It's miracles in everything.

Not every miracle is a huge showstopper. Look at your life. See the absolutely beautiful miracles you have in front of you, right now. Do you appreciate these ordinary miracles? Or do you take them for granted? By taking them for granted, you block more miracles from coming to you. When you live in gratitude for the miracles in your life, the Universe says, "Okay, that person wants more miracles in their life," and presto, more miracles come your way.

Try naming all the ordinary miracles in your life. Start a list in your journal right now of all those things you would describe as a miracle. It's time to appreciate the smallest of miracles and the biggest opportunities that lead you to the miracles. See everything, every experience, every person you meet as a miracle in your life.

You Are Always Manifesting

Move into visualizing, feeling, thinking, and speaking what it is you want. Know that what your mind can conceive, your life will display. Our life demonstrates our thoughts, our feelings, and our words. In other words, what we think, feel, and speak is what we create in our lives. We are manifesting all the time, intentionally or unintentionally, consciously or subconsciously.

It is more important now than ever to pay attention to how we express ourselves. There is tremendous fear in our world today. The collective consciousness carries fear about financial security, personal and national economic health, the nation's health care system, our physical well-being, our environment, even our social consciousness, our spiritual connection, and our relationships with ourselves and others on this planet. If we don't like the way our life reflects our thoughts back to us, then it is time to change our thoughts.

Our subconscious mind doesn't know the difference between real and fake. It grabs and holds on to whatever it is given. It's like a giant magnet that pulls what it believes closer and closer. It also accepts at face value what it is given. It does not judge. It is exactly like the Universe (or vice versa) in being impersonal and literal.

What do you feed your subconscious mind? What do you imagine? How do you see yourself? What do you believe, what do you feel, what do you visualize, and what do you speak? All of this moves right into your subconscious and demonstrates what it holds in your outer world. Do not forget your STOP light. Use it to eliminate your destructive negative thinking. Change takes practice and commitment, of course, but we know the reward is that our life will change for the better. It's worth the effort. Make a decision today, not for me, nor your spouse, nor your children, but for yourself, for your own better life experience.

If we come from negative thinking and negative talk, we will definitely be living with negativity. The words you speak today are the laws of your life. In the midst of crisis and life's challenges, we don't have the luxury of negative thinking. To move through the crisis and release the pain (whether it's emotional, physical, or mental), we must allow ourselves to move into the light and speak from the light. If you want light in all areas of your life, then *BE the light*.

You do not get what you pray for, you do not get what you ask for; *you get what you believe.*

Gratitude Empowers

"Give thanks for a little and you will find a lot."

—Hausa proverb from Nigeria

Gratitude is a state of mind. Gratitude empowers us. It heals our Soul. Take time each day to go to that place of gratitude.

I suggest you start listing your thoughts about gratitude in your journal. What are you grateful for? Start by listing the "small stuff," which is really the "big stuff." Having healthy food to eat, reliable transportation, a warm, dry home, a loving family, your pet, your friends, your income—these are good places to start. I speak of these as ordinary miracles. Each day, add one more gratitude to your list. Maybe you feel grateful that you can see a beautiful sunset. Maybe you're grateful for caller I.D. (one of my personal favorites). Express your gratitude to your Source every day. Acknowledge how blessed you are. This practice will change your life.

Do not wait for what you want your life to be before you practice gratitude. Be in gratitude *right where you are.* Claim your good and be grateful for it as if you already have it. Maintaining a constant knowledge of your good will bring you more good. Having a constant "attitude of gratitude" is being conscious that we are indeed provided for by the Source of All That Is in all areas of our lives. Jesus Christ said, "It is done unto you as you believe."

Are you grateful about where you are at this very moment in your life? Are you at peace in your present circumstances? When we speak our gratitude to the Universe, we must speak it with enthusiasm, as though our prayers have already been answered. You see, God already knows what you subconsciously believe and has already said, "Yes."

I had a client who was entrenched in her negativity and had great difficulty releasing it. When I brought up the necessity of living in gratitude and voicing our thanks every day, she said, "I speak my gratitude every morning when I wake up. I say, 'Thanks for this sh--ty day!'" And from her reports, that is exactly what she perceives her life to be.

Of course it may not seem possible to change some things in our life. If that's where you are, then focus your attention on what you can change *right now*. You can change your thinking about your circumstances at this moment. You can change your thoughts about your childhood right now. You have the power of choice at every moment. Choose different thinking. Continue to give thanks.

Tithing

I see tithing as an act of gratitude to my Source. I want God to know how grateful I am for my life and It's presence in all aspects of my life. I give the energy of love, in the form of money, to God, not to a building or a person. God shows Itself to me in multiple ways, as God is in and through all things. One way to demonstrate gratitude is by tithing where we receive our spiritual nourishment. What do I mean by *spiritual nourishment*? I am referring to spiritual inspiration, messages, and Divine presence.

In 2003, Edwene Gaines, minister, prosperity teacher, and president of The Masters' School in Alabama, visited our center to conduct a workshop on abundance and prosperity. I thought I knew everything about abundance, as I had been working on and teaching these philosophies for years. I attended the workshop to support my spiritual center. Little did I know that this workshop would change my life.

I learned from this spiritual teacher that tithing is about gratitude. Spiritual tithing is about giving ten percent of your gross (not your net) income to that place where you receive your spiritual food. This place can be your church, your synagogue, your spiritual center, or a representative of the Divine.

Tithe means "to give a tenth." You may be gasping at the thought of giving ten percent right off the top, before expenses. At first, it was difficult for me to wrap my mind around that, too. However, once I understood the spiritual meaning of tithing, I released my fears. To me, tithing really pertains to circulation, an abundance consciousness and gratitude to God.

By the end of that class, I had made a decision to immediately start tithing. I choose to tithe on a weekly basis. I will admit that when I wrote my first few tithe checks, it was a little scary. I was taking a huge step forward on my path of abundance. All the weeks, months, and years since that class and that first check have been completely easy.

It's all about circulation. As we give, so shall we receive. As I moved deeper and deeper into gratitude, the more my abundance flowed. At the end of that business year, my profit had increased by fifteen percent. Not only was my original tithe given back to me by the Universe, but I also received an additional five percent. Amazing! I didn't tithe in order to make money, but that's exactly what happened. Source always takes care of us when we live in alignment with the Universal Laws. What we give gratitude for, we get more of from the Divine Energy of God.

After you first tithe to that place where you receive your spiritual nourishment, then you can give to charities if you choose. I learned from Ms. Gaines's class that when we give in fear, we create more fear in our lives. Tithing is not about trying to get on God's good side. Tithing is about sharing the love in your heart and the gratitude of spiritual connection. If you choose to give to charitable organizations, do so after your spiritual tithe.

Affirmational Prayer

God is the full expression of life. At every moment of every day, God breathes good into my life. I trust this Truth and accept the knowing that I am the creative expression of God. I am one of God's miracles. I know my Soul. I AM one with my Soul.

I easily manifest powerful thoughts and beliefs. I hold the Truth. I open myself to Divine abundance in this very moment. Complete, radiant health, happiness, and financial blessings flow easily into my life.

I am grateful for expected and unexpected blessings. I freely share my wealth, and I am blessed in return. I allow my love to circulate with God's love, as we are One.

My gratitude extends out to all of God's creation. I release my words into the Universal Divine Mind, and it is done, it is done, it is done now.

And so it is. Amen

FORGIVENESS

Forgiveness Is a Gift

Forgiveness is the essence of Love. It comes from strength. The weak never forgive. Forgiveness is a gift you give yourself. You cannot truly forgive another person until you forgive yourself first. Forgiveness happens a step at a time, on every step of our journey. We need to keep forgiving.

BARBARA

Barbara, age eighty-one, often speaks of dying, although now she appears to be relatively well. Once, not long ago, when the subject of dying came up, I suggested she might consider moving into forgiveness to those she has held grudges against for so many years. This idea did not appeal to her. She was not open to the idea of forgiving. She listened as I suggested she begin with self-forgiveness, which then might lead her to be receptive to forgive one person in particular—her ex-husband, Peter, against whom she has held negative feelings for almost four decades. But when I mentioned this possibility, she exclaimed, "NO, I will never forgive him!" I shared the importance of identifying anything she might have contributed to the situation and that forgiving herself and then Peter, would allow her to move into peacefulness in her life and might even help improve her health. She became more and more upset at the idea and adamantly told me, "NO, NEVER!" She went on to recount all the ways she believed he had hurt her. She insisted on holding on to her deep anger and resentment. To this day, she completely blames her old relationship for her unhappiness and continuing depression.

Family History

The interaction I had with Barbara reminded me of the story of my maternal grandmother's anger toward her estranged sister. I believe that unresolved anger and inability to forgive probably contributed to my grandmother's early death at age sixty-one. Grandma took this anger to her grave.

Here's the story. Many years before her death, I heard my grandmother say, "I do not want my sister to come to my funeral. If she stands over my body, I will sit up and punch her in the face." I never met my great aunt, but this image and my grandmother's voice stayed in my young mind for years.

When the inevitable arrived and my grandmother died, the whole family wondered if her sister would dare to show up at the funeral. She did. When I saw my great aunt for the first time, I could see the strong sibling resemblance to my grandmother. They could have been twins. I had no doubt who she was. Aunt Alice walked into the funeral home and without saying a word to anyone, strolled right up to her sister's casket. Was Grandma really going to sit up and punch her? I held my breath. I could feel the whole family watching. Grandma's sister looked down onto her sister's face.

I was in my early twenties at the time and knew better, but my grandmother was so adamant in her anger that I wouldn't have been surprised if she had sat up and smacked her sister a good one. To this day, I don't know what the story between them was. But it really doesn't matter. Many members of my family still stubbornly refuse to forgive and let go of resentments. Many, many years have gone by, and the siblings still refuse to speak to one another. It seems a waste of time to tell them not to go to bed angry when they choose to die angry.

Where Are Your Wounds?

What do I mean by "wounds"? Our wounds are the unhealed places where emotional and physical trauma and hurts are held within our body, mind, and Soul. Our Soul's desire is to grow and change, not to stay stuck in what has kept it from living fully in this moment.

Do you self-medicate by covering up your feelings—your wounds—with Band-Aids like drugs, alcohol, overeating, shopping, sexual addiction, TV watching, Internet games, porn, smoking, sugar, or any other self-destructive behavior? Are you teaching and role modeling to your children or grandchildren how to live in wounded-ness?

There are positive ways to self-medicate. These include spirituality, exercise, meditation, yoga, walking, dancing, singing, reading self-help and inspirational books, music, art, creativity, volunteering, serving in your community, and advancing your knowledge, to name only a few.

Peel back the layers of your life, look at your wounds, and see how they display themselves. These wounds must be healed. It is not easy to feel our wounds or to look at the ugliness of a wound, but it is necessary to heal them if we want to move into a peaceful place. Intention is good, but it's not enough. It is the BE-ing *forgiving* that creates change. Show up in your own life!

Do You REALLY Want to Change?

Nothing is forever except change. Are you willing to do what is necessary to effect change in your life? Are you willing to face your demons (fears) and release them? How would your life be different if you really allowed change to take root in your life? How would that feel?

When you plant the seeds for real change it's important to have faith that what you plant will take root, sprout, and show itself in your life. The key is to understand that what you plant will always grow. If you plant corn, do not expect tomatoes to show up.

Negative thoughts will grow into "weeds" that choke out your dreams of happiness, abundance, and vitality. If you plant beautiful thought seeds, you will create beauty in all its forms. Your life will be rich and overflowing with more good than you can ever imagine.

There are those who claim they want change but are unwilling to leave the past behind. They can't seem to stop worrying about tomorrow. They often say, "I try, but…," or, "I know, but…," or, "I can't …," or, "I am cursed," or, "I am not good enough," or, "The world is against me." As they claim their inability to create something different, they are killing the beauty their Soul wants to move into. Do you find pleasure in negativity, fear, and continual drama?

LINDA

As a refugee of the 1994 genocide in Rwanda, Linda was sent to the southwest United States with two very young children in tow. She learned to speak English and moved to a town where she eventually found work, but not inner peace.

As a war widow carrying trauma and fear deep in her mental, emotional, and body memory, Linda is never really happy. After almost twenty years, she still carries her past with her. She refuses to speak of the atrocities of the genocide and that she witnessed her loved ones being slaughtered. Her pain and trauma are so deep, they do not allow her to sleep through the night. Unless we have gone through a similar experience; we won't be able to comprehend Linda's terror and emotional pain.

She has sabotaged numerous relationships and friendships because her irrational, obsessive, negative thoughts keep her terrified that people will abandon her, do not really love her, will lie to her, will cheat on her, and will steal from her. Linda lives in a fantasy world of romance novels, movies, cigarette smoking, caffeine, alcohol, abusive verbal behavior, and isolating herself from others.

In 2006, Linda married her third husband, who loved her tremendously, but because she carried so much fear and belief of unworthiness she continually planted seeds of anger. Anger is what showed up as the couple had countless arguments and separations. She verbally, emotionally, and physically pushed him away, until he finally couldn't take it any longer. Then she blamed him for leaving and not loving her. As she feared abandonment, she created abandonment as a result.

This continual spiral of self-abuse and self-defeating behavior makes Linda more negative and unhappy. She refuses to seek help of any kind. She says she wants to change, but she does nothing to move toward change. She and her husband divorced three years later. Linda is very aware of her pain and suffering, but chooses to live in denial that she must change. To find peace in her Soul the wounds she carries must heal.

Self-Forgiveness

It is said that our most important growth work is to first forgive ourselves so we can move more easily into forgiving others.

Our inner critical thoughts beat us up worse than any person's words could ever possibly do. Why do we allow ourselves to be our own worst critics? Self-judgment and recrimination seem to be part of the basis of our negative collective thinking. *As we think, so do we create.* The words we speak and the feelings we demonstrate are reflected back to us in our world. As others criticized and judged us, we may have internalized their words and claimed this negative information as our own.

We have all done things that we regret and are ashamed of. We hold those things we do not want others to know about inside us. Then we use them to beat ourselves up by allowing the ego to have its negative way with us. STOP internalizing others' negative talk. Do not agree with your negative self-talk! Remember that you are not your thoughts. Keep this negative voice away. Use your STOP light and talk back! Take action to break the chains of the ego. Exclaim to this egoic energy, *These lies are the thief of my happiness! I will not allow this negative thought and energy to be with me any longer. I know what you are doing, and I will not go there with you. I am a child of the Divine, and I am loved. God accepts me just as I AM.* Use your STOP light and fill the silence with loving self-thoughts.

Go to your journal again and start a new page. What

has not and is not working for you? What pain and anger are you holding on to? List ten (or more) issues that you are willing to release right now.

No matter what has happened to you in the past, no matter what you have done in the past, it is *in the past*. Do not allow the past to invade your present life. Let it go and enjoy this moment of silence, peace, and happiness. When you pay attention to your inner thoughts, stop the negative thinking, and replace them with positive statements, you will feel lighter and freer.

Ephesians 6:14 says, *"Put on the breastplate of God's favor."* This means you should protect yourself from the accuser (the ego, inner negative thinking) by knowing that you are loved and protected by God.

Does God Always Forgive?

Actually, God does not believe we are wrong, bad, sinners, or failures. For this reason, God does not believe there is anything to forgive. God bestows unconditional love upon us, no matter what we do. Only man judges.

You may have started asking for forgiveness ten years ago, and every day you are still asking God for forgiveness. The challenge is not in God not forgiving you, however; it is in YOU not forgiving yourself. You see, God has held you in the energy of forgiveness for the last ten years, from the moment you asked. While ego still blames, God ACCEPTS you with unconditional love.

Release your guilt and condemnations. The Divine

One focuses on what is good about you, not on your past mistakes. You have to release that old "poor me" victim mentality. Release self-pity and forgive yourself.

Do You Like Yourself?

You must also release self-hate. The closest relationships you will ever have is your relationship with your God and with yourself. *Liking* yourself is as important as loving yourself. If you both like and love yourself, your life will seem easier. Remember that Universal Love is always with you, no matter what the outward appearance is.

Did it seem that your parents liked and loved themselves? Were they good role models of self-love, or did they demonstrate spiritual separation and fear-based behavior?

Personal experience is everything. If your parents were not held or told they were loved when they were children, they didn't learn how to demonstrate physical and emotional affection to you. This was the case in my family.

My elderly mother cried when she spoke of her childhood. She was born the middle child to her eighteen-year-old mother and her forty-four-year-old father, who was often ill. My maternal grandmother born to interracial parents. Her father (my great grandfather) moved to America directly from England. My great grandmother was Cherokee Indian (a fact my mother hid until the day she died). My maternal grandfather was born in Germany. Not only the cultures, but also the generations embraced stoicism and a strong work ethic. Both my great grandparents and their children (my grandparents) lacked experience in the verbal and physical affection that children thrive on. Therefore, my mother also lacked that experience.

I was born during World War II, the oldest child with two younger brothers. I know my mother loved us, cared for us, and provided for us, but she had no idea how to tell us she loved us and never showed physical affection. When I was forty years old and just starting on my spiritual journey, I realized I had no memory of being held as a child. Yes, I was carried from one place to another, of course, but I was not held and hugged. Not until she was much older was my mother able to say, "I love you."

Unfortunately, when my son was born, I, too, was disconnected from demonstrating physical and verbal affection. Once I realized what I was lacking, however, I changed, though the changes came slowly. Today my son, grandsons, friends, and family reap the rewards of my healing.

I am grateful as I witness my son's loving behavior with his sons. From their birth, he has told them he loves them and easily gives hugs and kisses. Our family's generational dysfunction and fear of loving affection have been broken.

You need to love yourself in the midst of challenges. It is important to release self-pity. Once we have an understanding of a possible cause of our lack of self-love, we can let it go. Consider NOT having to know what caused your block and let it go, anyway. The message is about releasing and letting go of what was...*whatever it was.*

Claim this day as a new day. Start fresh. Remember the old saying, "This is the first day of the rest of your life." Act on this knowledge. Move past that thought and know this is the ONLY day of your life. Right here, right now, this is it.

It's time to like, love, and forgive yourself so you can really be present in loving others. It's impossible to give what you don't have. When you finally realize and absorb the truth of what you have, whether you know it consciously or not, your life will change.

You have the Source's unconditional love with no strings attached. God's great pleasure is to take care of you, heal you, and give you more than you now believe is possible. All you have to do is live in gratitude, open to receive your good, and believe you deserve it. When you learn the power of forgiveness, you will also learn the power of freedom. It's life-changing to let go of the old destructive, negative thinking. This work is for your personal well-being, not someone else's. Learn how to detach from others' choices and respect their journeys. You will definitely be happier for it. Don't allow your family's history to dictate your behavior. Choose Love!

A Forgiveness Ceremony

It is important to create a sacred space for your forgiveness ceremony. Light candles and burn incense. Play peaceful music and invoke divine energy into your space. Think about the people and circumstances that you have not truly, deeply forgiven. Now set your intention to release and claim this release as a growth opportunity that will let change enter into your heart and your life.

Be specific as you list your perceptions of troublesome events in your life. Be specific about the grudges you may hold. How did the events affect your life when they happened? Who else was involved? What do you wish you had done differently? How do you feel your life might have turned out if you had made a different choice?

Now write an apology to yourself, a letter of forgiveness to yourself for making mistakes or bad decisions. Forgive yourself for holding on to grudges and the negative energy of anger. Tell yourself that you are not bad. Consider that it's just possible that your choice was not a mistake, but was based on what you needed to learn and experience at that time. Remember, God does not blame you for your choices. You have been given free will. God does not judge or need to forgive anyone for anything. In God's eyes, the situation was over and done with a long, long time ago.

End the self-blame. Stop blaming any other person involved. No one says this is easy. Remember, however, that it is essential to your well-being and personal growth to release and let go of that which no longer serves you.

Now write a letter to the person against whom you hold hatred, anger, and resentment. As you write, you are practicing detachment from what you feel was "done" to you. Know your Soul chose circumstances and experiences to give you the opportunity to forgive and love. Write about the experiences that upset you and how they made you feel.

Fully express all your negativity and how you have allowed it to affect your life. Feel what parts of your body are being affected now as you allow the old feelings to surface and be released through your writing. Rant and rave all you want. Write as many pages as it takes. Take as long as you need to. This is a process. You will find that it's easier than you thought to move into a place of forgiveness, not only of yourself, but also of the other person.

This letter is not meant to be sent to the person you're writing to. This is for your own personal growth and healing. Put it in your journal. Reread your letter. Take a deep breath. If more energy needs to be released...write some more. Keep writing.

When you feel complete, you may decide to tear the letter to shreds. You may want to burn it or bury it. You may decide to keep it in your journal to reread sometime in the future, to witness where you used to be. But it's not at all necessary to hang on to these letters.

Use this letter-writing ceremony for every person and issue you need to forgive. Your release process will be of tremendous help to you when you remember that the people you held anger toward are simply Souls on their own personal journeys, just as you are. They're learning their lessons at the speed and level that's right for them at any given time. Choice is key here. You are in choice of forgiveness, or not, all the time.

Love Your Inner Self-Child!

In the early 1980s, I joined the inner child recovery movement. I have never stopped engaging in this relationship with myself. In those early days, the information taught came mainly from a psychological viewpoint. Through many years of self-development, I was inspired to create a compilation of methods, to which I added my own ideas as I developed a very effective program of spiritually-based inner-child discovery and recovery that becomes a journey to deep self-love. I have been teaching this method, which I call the *Five-Step Journey to Healing the Wounded Warrior* program, to clients since 1994. The "wounded warriors" are the disowned, unloved, abandoned, abused, or unknown aspects of ourselves. They do their best to survive, but come from an immature, fearful, and sometimes lost place.

Through the years, clients would tell me they had previously taken a class in inner-child work, but did not continue practicing what they learned. It is no wonder, then, that they still demonstrate and experience a lack of self-love. The whole point of developing a healthy relationship with yourself is to continue having a healthy relationship with yourself for the rest of your life!

Self-love is a spiritual endeavor. As we love our Source, so do we love ourselves, and therefore we can truly love others. We can only give what we have. Nothing else matters but Love. We will do anything for love.

Just because our body grows up, this does not necessarily mean our emotions grow up, too. I call our emotions "inner children" to help simplify our understanding the importance of identifying, getting in touch with, and interacting with all aspects of ourselves. This does not mean we are living in the past, It means we are helping the wounded aspects of ourselves to heal in the present.

Have you ever experienced a spontaneous emotional regression in which you feel like a child when someone has said something hurtful to you? You may burst into tears and feel five years old again. You may go to anger, to fear, even to feeling like you've been punched in the gut when something or someone triggers this reaction.

Our wounds are demonstrated by our uncomfortable emotions. If we still carry a great deal of childhood trauma, we may often act out through childish emotions. That doesn't mean that when our wounds are healed we will not be childlike. Having a childlike, magical quality is part of the fun of life. Remember your happiest childhood moments. It's possible that if there are no memories of good times, maybe there weren't many happy moments.

People are often so immersed in their work, dealing with stress, and just surviving that they don't even remember how to be silly, have fun, and be childlike. Do you remember how to play? Did your parents engage in play with you when you were a child? Do you and your family play with the children? Do you engage in wonderful, creative activities that nourish not only your inner-child's self, but also your grown-up self?

I do not have childhood memories of adults spending playtime with me. My father was absent, and my mother was emotionally detached and working hard. She had no time for play. I never had a tea party. Mostly, I played alone. I learned to be very creative and made up games to play with my younger brothers, but they were more interested in playing boy games than playing with their sister. When I was playing alone, I made mud pies, created my own songs and games, and played with paper dolls until they fell apart.

If this sounds or feels familiar to you, it may be time to get in touch with your own inner child. Our emotions are God-given gifts and not to be denied. Your family dynamic may also have been one of stoicism, so your emotions were neither honored nor respected. Maybe the dynamic in your home was chaotic, and everyone's emotion was displayed without discernment. Or perhaps there was abuse in your childhood and you learned to withdraw, detach, and live in fear.

As you revisit your role models' (your primary caretakers) ability (or lack of ability) to show their feelings in a healthy way, write in your journal about your childhood memories and the feelings you associate with the experiences. Give yourself permission to experience a wide range of emotions. Release your fears and tears as you document both challenging and fond memories.

Suffering and pain must be healed. If you feel your wounds are still deep and are sabotaging your wellness, seek professional help to witness and move forward into healing the wounded warrior.

Nurturing Self

As we learn to love ourselves unconditionally, we will feel a stronger desire for self-nurturing. It is not being "selfish" to be kind to yourself. The more loving and present we are in our Being, the more loving and present we are able to be with others. We teach others how to treat us. Others treat us as we treat ourselves. Those who are codependent and put themselves second, or last, will eventually hold resentments.

How would you grade your level of self-worth? Is it based on what others think of you? Are you treated with respect? Do you feel heard? Do you think others look down on you? Do you feel judged or criticized? Have you forgiven yourself? Maybe you're projecting to others the feelings you carry about yourself. Be kind to yourself. Love and forgive yourself. Remember that in God's heart you are unique and the most wonderful Being in the world!

Energy

You are responsible for the energy you bring into every situation. What do you contribute to the energy on the planet? What energy do you bring to other people? Do you bring love or hate? Joy or pain? Do you spend your time with energy drainers? Do you drain other people's energy? You drain other people's energy when you are negative and critical.

Are you operating from an attached place? To be attached is to be critical and judgmental of others, possibly because of their gender, their race, their culture, their beliefs, their sexual orientation, their financial status, their address, their vehicle, their age, their physical appearance, their height, or their weight. You are attached when you feel no sympathy, empathy, or compassion. You are empty of compassion, but filled with ego.

It is said that *when we are attached to anything we are disconnected from God.* God does not attach to anything. If God were attached, our planet would be a very different place to live. Think about it. God is impersonal, therefore detached from our choices. That doesn't mean IT doesn't care and love us. It means IT does not judge us. We judge ourselves and each other. God is as connected to us, as we are to IT.

Everything is energy. We are all made up of energy. Who has not witnessed the misuse of energy on this planet? What we do with our own energy is our responsibility. We must pay attention to what we create in our life, our relationships, and our world. What energy do you emanate into the consciousness of the human race?

You are a part of this world. Maybe you do not believe in Souls. Maybe you do not believe in God. Okay, fine. However, you have a responsibility to be a part of the planet as a conscious human being. You have an obligation to be the best human being you can be, one who causes no harm to others. You are responsible for your own beliefs, actions, attitudes, and behaviors.

Write in your journal how you are or are not being responsible to yourself, your life, and your planet. Are you being environmentally conscious? Are you respectful of the Souls on this planet? Are you bringing peace to the collective consciousness on the planet, or are you bringing fear? Are you living your life *on purpose*, with inner awareness? Take a closer look. Lift the Band-Aids and look closely at your wounds.

Affirmational Prayer

God's radiant light penetrates and permeates all things. This very space is filled with the presence of the One Mind. I take responsibility for what I contribute to this One Mind.

My body pulsates with energy of life. My every breath is an expression of God in form. Every cell of my body glows with healing, vibrant, abundant, and joyous blessings of Good. I embrace the Truth of who I AM, my Soul, a beloved child of the One Source. I am the favored child.

As God honors me, I honor my Being, and I honor my Soul. As God loves me unconditionally, I love myself unconditionally! My Soul sings. Gratitude fills my thoughts, my feelings, and vibrates through my essence as I release my prayer-filled intentions to forgive myself, change, and to surrender to my Source all that does not serve my Soul. The Universe accepts this affirmation into the Law and circulates this powerful expression of Good back into my life, endlessly.

All is Good. All is God.
All is Light. All is Love.
It is received *now*.
And so it is.
Amen.

TRUTH, LIES, AND FAIRY TALES

Fear of the Truth

There is a difference between truth and Truth. In my opinion, lowercase-t truth is what the negative ego believes. It's a personal interpretation of something and it can be filled with misconceptions and opinions based on false beliefs. When someone speaks their lowercase-t truth from their own understanding, it can carry the fear energy and therefore not be in alignment with their God-self or the Truth of Divine thinking and mindfulness. Truth with an uppercase T is when energy is aligned with Source.

My truth may be different from your truth. However, God's Truth is always the same. There is One Universal Truth. There is One Universal Mind. Practice speaking the Truth, even when it is uncomfortable. We must practice hearing the uncomfortable Truth. I can speak and hold Truth for myself and for you, and you can speak and hold

Truth for yourself and others. When we reside in the light of Truth, the world makes a little more sense.

Our perceptions and misconceptions, usually based in fear, keep us from the real Truth and the principles of Universal Law. Ego must step aside so that you can hear and speak God's Truth. However, ego fears God's Truth and it will lie and manipulate to keep you unaware and imprisoned. How can we be authentic if we do not see, know, and speak the Truth? Open your heart to Truth.

In this country, we all have our own opinions and the freedom to speak our beliefs. Our freedom is sacred. When we speak of the differences in types of truth, I would like to clarify that we definitely are free to own what feels right and true for us.

I now speak my Truth: *Trusting God's Truth of unconditional love, complete abundance, and happiness as being right in front of me, all around me, and moving through me and as me, will create a life of peace and joy beyond my imagination.*

You may speak this Truth as your Truth too. It is the Truth for all of us. Claim your Truth, own your Truth, and speak your Truth.

God denies that evil, disease, and lack exist, for if God acknowledged that these negative elements existed, God would be a part of the negativity. God knows NO-thing of negativity, but does not judge us if we choose to live in It. Challenges of negativity are simply appearances coming from a belief that one is separate from God. If we believe things come at us, attach to us, and happen to us, we will feel powerless in our victimhood. Personal darkness cannot exist in the Light of the Divine. There is deep Truth in the Universal Law of Attraction. We draw to us what we believe.

Stand in Your Truth

A core teaching in Religious Science[21] is that *God works in Truth*. What is your Truth? Are you accountable to your Truth? Do you feel the need to defend your Truth? It may sometimes feel as if you do, but often, the more you defend your opinions, the more others stop listening. Nevertheless, I believe it is very important to stand in your Truth. This is not an easy thing to do. You may not receive approval from others when you speak the Truth of the Source. You can change the world by standing up for your Truth. Are you willing to take that chance? Trust YOUR Truth.

There are "yes" people who flow with the wind of current belief. Some may call them politicians. Some may call them fearful or self-serving. They may appear ungrounded and unsure of themselves, looking for guidance instead of creating a potentially new path. I believe Jesus was creating a new path and challenging those who were fearful "yes" people.

Why are we afraid of speaking the Truth? Because it brings forward the possibility of ridicule, judgment, and criticism. It may bring up fears, as we remember what

---

21 Religious Science, or Science of Mind, founded by Ernest Holmes in the 1920s, is a spiritually based system and part of the New Thought movement that teaches belief in Oneness and Affirmative Prayer.

happened to Jesus Christ, Mahatma Gandhi, and Martin Luther King Jr., among others, for speaking their Truth.

There is the collective consciousness that is holding fear of the Christian persecutors and tortures during the Holy Inquisition that lasted about 800 years.[22] This is the longest holocaust in the history of the world.[23] Many feel that "it is safer to go with the crowd" and stay quiet and invisible. Keep in mind that what we hold fear of, we draw into our life. Remember God's promise in Isaiah 54:7, *"No enemy set against you can ever prosper."*

Stay focused and centered in your spiritual practice and awareness that God moves through you and as you. Nothing can come between you and your God. Truth always prevails. God is Truth and Truth is God. Being Truthful in all your relationships builds trust and respect. This also means self-respect. Truth always eventually surfaces, doesn't it? Be an example of Truth. As you speak and live your Truth, you will become a light that shines the way for others to walk the path of Truth, Love, and Shining Light.

Have compassion in the Truth process. Choosing our words consciously when delivering Truth is always a good idea. Tact and Truth make good partners. As a direct, honest, and Truthful person, I have learned to be more tactful than I was in my younger years. I used to be tactless. I didn't realize that what I was saying, even though I thought it was true, could hurt someone's feelings. I chose my words

---

22   Helen Ellerbe, *The Dark Side of Christian History* (Morningstar & Lark, 1995).

23   *The Horrors of the Church and Its Holy Inquisition* www. bibliotecapleyades.net/vatican/esp_vatican29.htm#The Church

more carefully today. In my Truth and fierce integrity, do I miss the compassion? In the compassion, do I sacrifice integrity? No, I do not believe so. Not anymore. Awareness of the words we speak is being responsible for the energy we bring into the world. We cannot make someone else feel what they are not willing to feel. Be an aware and conscious individual and do not purposely "push others' buttons." When you know that negative, unaware behavior is your ego acting out, you can stop the behavior before it affects others.

Where is the value in Truth? When we live in the consciousness of the Universal Principles[24], that is, the Truth, we can witness everything more clearly.

Lies

Gossip magazines are filled with lies. The news media perpetrate lies. The social media also perpetrate lies. The government operates on lies. Corporate America was built on lies. Organized religion is often based on lies and fear. Big Pharma and the drug companies refuse to tell the truth. The tobacco companies lied to us for years.

The negative collective consciousness holds on to all these lies. Why do people lie? Lying is one form of manipulation. Ego lies, but God does not lie. Our Soul does not lie!

The need to lie, deceive, and exaggerate is fear-based.

---

24   *Universal Cosmic Law, The Seven Principles,* http://www.pymander.com/AETHEREAL/PRINC~1.html

Whether it is low self-esteem, competition, greed, seeking attention, or an unawareness of the negative energy of speaking untruths into the Universe, it certainly creates an imbalance in one's self and all relationships.

We would like to think that we would not find fear and lies in religious organizations. Unfortunately, the ancient collective consciousness of fear in and of the church still prevails.

ANNE

Anne wanted to serve her New England church community as it was going through a major leadership change, so she volunteered to sit on a search committee. As the ministerial selection process, which started out with a cohesive group of like-minded people, moved along its path, Anne learned that many of the selection committee members and the church's board of directors were in great fear of change and conflict. Choosing fear, they lost their integrity.

Here's the story that Anne shared with me. The search for a new minister began when the founding minister retired and relocated. During the interval between the old and new ministers, Elmer, a minister-in-training, was asked to fill in and help hold the community together during the transition. He gave messages on Sundays. Anne and most other members of the church liked Elmer and were glad for his support. However, as he became aware that the committee was moving forward in the selection process, Elmer became antagonistic, fear-based, ego-ruled, defensive, and destructive to this church community. He acted out and spread rumors and lies about the leaders in the church, the selection committee, and other congregants. A few people believed him, but the majority did not. This split the community. Whether this was self-sabotage on Elmer's part or not, no one knows.

Anne told me that she saw the mentality of the church leaders as in denial and not wanting to be bothered with scheduling a flow of visiting ministers. They preferred to take the proverbial easy road and continue to accept Elmer's presence, no matter how destructive it was. The board of directors felt they owed him the opportunity to also be a candidate for the open position of resident minister.

Several months into the selection process, Elmer was licensed as a minister. The committee received his resume and a request from him to be considered for this important position. All of the candidates had to go through a screening process that began with an interview. Those who passed the interview were invited to present a Saturday workshop and a Sunday message, plus attend social gatherings with the selection committee and the board members.

The congregation also had the opportunity to attend meetings where they could ask questions and get to know the potential new ministers. Because Elmer had been speaking each Sunday for almost a year, many church attendees bonded with him. He used this to his advantage and continued his unethical behavior in an effort to manipulate the decision of the committee.

After they uncovered lies on Elmer's resume, they knew that he was not qualified to fill the important leadership role. The discrepancies on his resume were brought to the attention of the board of directors, along with a recommendation to eliminate Elmer as a potential ministerial candidate. But the president of the board refused to make a change. He stayed in denial of the damage being done to the church community. Fearful of looking foolish for making this huge mistake, the board president refused to stop Elmer's candidacy.

When Anne shared her feelings about the injustice and the board's denial of the situation with the committee, she was told to "get past it," and to "keep your mouth shut." This lack of courage on the part of the church leaders and their refusal to take a stand on behalf of the church community, had Anne feeling unheard and discounted.

Anne recognized the fears she felt as old, so old, she knew they came through from past lifetimes of religious abuse, ostracizing, killings, tortures, burnings, lies, injustice, and misplaced loyalty. The church leaders' voices she was hearing sounded extremely familiar to her. Who was suffering this time? The congregation was suffering, the church leadership was suffering, the consciousness and integrity of all the members of the committee and board were suffering. They were all afraid of looking foolish. They were afraid to admit they were wrong about Elmer. The church was misusing its power and pursuing ego-based, political behavior. Not understanding the truth of what was happening, the congregation suffered for almost a year, and still Anne refused to stop speaking her Truth. She brought the Truth forward to anyone who would listen to her. Not many would listen.

The selection committee finally made its choice for the ministerial position. The chosen one was an experienced minister from another state. When Elmer learned of this decision, his negative behavior escalated. He recruited his followers, called the powers in charge, and had Anne "fired" from her volunteer position on the selection committee because she was a "troublemaker." She felt humiliated, betrayed, and abandoned by the church board and selection committee, who did not back her up. Those people who did not stand in Truth said one thing in their meetings and another to Elmer and the congregation. But they really weren't fooling anyone. They were demonstrating unethical behavior, lack of integrity, and misplaced loyalty.

Anne was facing a choice. She chose to move into forgiveness. Forgiving herself for bringing this drama into her life was her first step. She also had to move into forgiveness for those who asked her to step down from the selection committee because she wouldn't remain quiet. She had to grieve the loss of the trust and respect she had had for the leaders of the church. She had to grieve the loss of her church community.

The experience helped her heal many issues from past lifetimes related to politics in the church. Her fears had to surface in order for her Soul to grow. She worked to forgive those people involved for the demonstration of their denial, fears, and guilt, knowing it was okay for them to be where they were on their Soul path.

Truth always surfaces. Truth prevails. Truth is the cement of our spiritual foundation. If we continue to turn our backs on the Truth, how can we expect history and the collective consciousness to change?

You may have witnessed politics in your own church community. All churches are businesses. Where ever there is a system in place to run a business, we will see politics. I believe it is simply human nature (ego) showing its desire to control and promote its own agenda. We all know of many religious organizations and traditions that don't want to hear our thoughts about the way they run their business or the beliefs they preach. So, out of fear, people keep their mouths shut.

Just because it is a church community should not mean you don't have the right to speak your Truth, question their teachings, and pay attention to how the leaders of the church community are spending your money and what they are teaching your children.

Claim your personal power and find out where the lies are buried.

Judgment

It is said in the New Testament that Jesus taught, *"Judge not, that ye be not judged"* (Matthew 7:1). When we judge others, we are really bringing judgment upon ourselves. Our inner critical mind-stuff can endlessly speak judgment in our lives, which then demonstrates outwardly unless we surrender those thoughts immediately into the Universal Law of cause and effect.

Cause and effect are about balance. What we sow, we must reap. This is a natural process, not a weapon used by God as a punishment or judgment. The impersonal mind of the Universe always grants us what we believe and speak about.

When you're aware of negative self-talk (cause), the ego will be diminished by the very act of your awareness (effect). Therefore, when you are aware of judgment and criticism of self or others, you must immediately cancel the thought (use your STOP light) and replace it with a kind and loving thought. Catch yourself as quickly as you can and change the energy you put out into the world. The ego cannot live in the Light of your awareness.

Curses

When negative words are spoken over another person, it's sometimes said that that person has been cursed or condemned. We see this in every culture, community, and tradition. Why? Because everyone on the planet has a fear-based ego. The fear-based ego in all its negativity, wants everyone to suffer. When you hold others in a thought of *not good enough*, or *not smart enough* or *not deserving*, you are thinking of them or seeing them in a dark place.

Family members may have spoken condemnation over you, and you may be speaking these same curses over your children and your relationships. Listen to what you're saying. You have the power to STOP condemning and cursing others.

Clients have shared with me their fears of their loved ones not being happy, not finding employment, and not finding healthy relationships. They are focused on what is *wrong* in their family's lives. This worry and fear is the same thing as placing a curse on someone. They are speaking lack and negativity into their loved ones' lives. Remember, what we focus our attention on, we create more of.

When you have a concern for a loved one, go into your heart center, connect with your god, and actively send a prayer of gratitude for that which you want to see in their life. Here is an example of such a prayer:

Dearest Beloved Source, thank you for reminding me to pray over my loved one. I surrender all my worry and concern for my loved one's choices to you. I know you protect, support, and supply all that [she/he] needs and wants. I trust that [she/he] is continuously watched over by you. I see the bright light of the Universe surrounding [her/his] body, mind, soul, home, transportation, financial security, and all areas of [her/his] life. I am in gratitude for the unending good in [her/his] life. Thank you, God. Amen.

It is your responsibility as a member of the human race consciousness to hold your fellow human in the Light. Help to raise them up by knowing they are favored by the loving God just as much as you are. You are no better or lesser than them. We are all ONE in the eyes of the Beloved.

Go to your journal and write all the curses you have heard directed toward you. Who ridiculed you? Who criticized you? Who said you could not do what you dreamed of doing? Now look at yourself. When, how, and whom do you criticize? Do you speak condemnation over any person, belief system, race, gender, sexual orientation, or culture? How does this make you feel? Take your time and let this journaling become a process of awareness and release. Allow change to happen.

Family Secrets

Secrets are toxic. Secrets make us sick. Where there are secrets, there are mountains of lies. Where there are secrets, there are shame and fear of rejection. Where secrets are buried, there are festering wounds.

During the dinner following my mother's memorial service, my aunt shared with me for the very first time that my mother's maternal grandmother had been a full-blooded Cherokee. First, I felt shock. "Why did my mother lie to me?" "Why didn't she tell us?"

This information is so important to who I am. As a child, I often asked my mother about our ancestry. Along with being told that her maternal grandfather was from England and her own father was from Germany, she briefly mentioned that "somewhere in the past there was an Indian in the woodpile." That statement made no sense to me. I had no idea what it meant. I was never given direct information.

I felt a deep loss in not knowing my true heritage. Now I feel honored to know I have this bloodline. My mother's fears and shame inhibited my discovery of my true self. With that being said, I have always felt a pull to the Native American culture. While seeking and discovering my spirituality, I often attended American Indian gatherings and pow-wows. I studied shamanism and attended power dances. I felt my bloodline calling, but I had no idea why.

Are there secrets in your family? Are you holding secrets from your family? How much pain has this caused you? How much pain has this caused others? As a child, were you told blatantly or subliminally, "Don't tell the family secrets" or "Don't air our dirty laundry in public" or "Keep the family secrets." I was.

My family did not model the virtue of ethics and integrity. Sadly, I can share here that my biological father was a child molester (to me when I was five), a thief, and a liar and that he spent time incarcerated for grand theft auto and writing bad checks. He was the black sheep of his family. My mother was a minor thief who thought it was funny to steal coffee mugs, small containers, and flatware, anything from restaurants that she could fit into her purse. My parents were certainly very poor examples for their children.

Of course I had to unlearn this behavior, but Truth, justice, and integrity have always been familiar Soul feelings in me. I have always been able to see the Truth beyond the illusions and beyond the veil of lies. Being intuitive, I can spot a falsehood pretty fast. Maybe that's why I repeatedly asked my mother about our heritage. I always felt there was something missing. I could feel the secrets and the lies.

My aunt told us many more family secrets that day at my mother's memorial dinner, but those are secrets I will not speak of at this time. They were shocking, yet not worthy of keeping as secrets and lies. It's good that all of our family members now know the truth.

The veil between Truth and lies is thin and transparent. So are the lies that liars tell. I suggest that you tell your family all the secrets you're holding. Nothing will be as painful as holding these toxic lies and secrets in your mind and body. Don't be a coward and leave this lifetime with your secrets. Don't leave your family to clean up your mess.

MARCIA

When I heard this story, it sounded all too familiar. Marcia's siblings did not see the lies perpetrated by their mother, who was a narcissistic personality and master manipulator who carried strong victim mentality. Marcia's sister, Laura, believed her mother's lies. The sisters never had a significant disagreement beyond childhood squabbles, but they never had real in-depth conversations, either. Even without arguing, they became estranged for fifteen years. How on earth did that happen?

Marcia's mother told lies to her about Laura, her brother-in-law, and their children. She could tell when her mother was lying, however, because she knew the truth about her sister. Marcia knew her sister's Soul. Her mother would also fabricate stories about Marcia to the family, and they all believed her. Being the mother, she found it easy to fool the family. She finally was able to manipulate them into believing Marcia was a terrible person. Laura and her family believed the lies and turned their backs on Marcia.

Although Laura lived in the same state and county as Marcia, she ignored all of Marcia's attempts to make connect. Believing the lies, she had no time for her older sister. Marcia phoned, wrote letters, and sent emails. No response for fifteen years. The only person who had contact with both sisters was the mother, who like a hub of a wheel seemed to have control over everyone.

Marcia was devastated. For many years after her "abandonment," she told me, she would wake up from nightmares gasping for air, in total panic with the pain of the loss of her sister. It took her ten years to grieve her sister's "death," for surely Laura was not coming back to her. The last five years of the fifteen-year separation, Marcia could finally get through the night without tears.

The lies perpetrated in her family extended out to her aunts and uncles and nieces and nephews. Marcia was the proverbial black sheep and scapegoat of the family.

When Marcia called her mother on her lies and bad behavior, her mother would wince, look at Marcia out of the corner of her eye, with an expression that said, "I will get even." She despised Marcia for speaking her truth. The rest of the family only saw the mother's mask, which was hiding the lies, whereas Marcia saw beneath the mask. She sometimes wished she could not see her mother's dark side.

And then Marcia's mother had a stroke which took away much of her speaking ability…and her ability to lie and manipulate the family. The Universe sometimes has an ironic sense of humor. The loss of speech, however, did not stop her mother's attempts to continue her negative behavior, for she was not yet aware that her mask had been removed. Now the family could no longer be deceived.

As Laura and her family eventually became aware of the lies about Marcia and were able to see what Marcia had always seen, communication opened between the sisters. Laura and Marcia reunited and swore never to believe lies about each other again and to always keep each other "in the loop" of Truth. They are now closer than ever and engage in deep conversations. They now see and bless their mother as who she is—a Soul on her own journey. The veil of lies has been removed. The healing between the sisters is beautiful.

Marcia's mother told lies. Cause and effect is always at work. We can only imagine what possible unhappiness that mother reaped. The lesson here is to choose your behavior wisely for it not only effects others, but comes right back to you.

As we sow, so shall we reap (Galatians, 6:7).

Fairy Tales and Fantasy in Relationships

As we have explored the black and white world of truth and lies, we need to ask, what about the gray area? Fairy tales and fantasy fall into the gray area. Sometimes it's difficult to realize we are living in a fantasy world.

What do you tell yourself when something or someone new comes into your life? Do you look at the truth, the Truth, or the what-ifs? Do you live in denial and illusion? Do you ignore red flags? Do you overlook what is right in front of you only to see what you want to believe? Do you think you can change another person? Do you want to "fix" them? Do you think that if they love you enough, they will change for you?

Not jumping into a decision immediately is a good idea. Maybe getting to know someone better before taking them into your life based on the fantasy of a long-term relationship is a better choice. This is not about living in fear. It's about discernment.

Typically, when we enter a relationship, we enter a fantasy of what it will be like to be friends with this person or be a partner with that person. What about living "happily ever after?" What does that really mean to you? Children read fairy tales. Fantasy is fun. Disneyland is a fantasy world and a great place to visit. But we wouldn't want to live there. When people live in a fantasy world on a daily basis, it sets them up for hard falls.

What were the fairy tales of your youth? Did your parents live in their own fantasyland? Did you escape into a fantasyland? Playing with dolls allowed me to escape a reality in which I was unhappy. Did you have an imaginary friend? What kind of games did you play? How did you create a different perception of your life? Are you still doing that? How? What do you do to self-comfort? Make a list in your journal and write what you understand now about the difference between fantasy, illusions, and reality.

Promises

What do promises mean to you? Do you honor your promises? Do you make and then break them? Have you experienced broken promises? How does it feel?

In my experience, broken promises feel like betrayal. A child will take a broken promise personally and wonder what's wrong with them. Children internalize what their parents model for them. Be mindful that you are a role model. Do not make a promise you cannot keep. Remember the Golden Rule.

Integrity

It's a challenge not to take broken promises personally. It hurts most when this behavior comes from a loved one. I take promises seriously. If I make one, I keep it. Of course, life has its unpredictable circumstances, but that is not what we are speaking of here. We are talking about integrity. Your level of integrity reflects who you are and whether you respect yourself and others. When you keep your promises you show integrity and gain respect. Respect is not a birthright. If you want to be respected, you must earn respect. When we set a date, an appointment with a friend or a family member, keep it. And show up on time. Build your personal integrity and respect by keeping promises.

ELLEN

Several years ago, I met Ellen through a mutual friend and we enjoyed antiquing together. After a few months of sharing time, however, she began canceling our luncheons or shopping trips at the last minute, always with the excuse that she had a headache. If Ellen was the one who suggested getting together, doing what she wanted to do, she was fine. Cancellations happened when I made the plans.

One day I asked her to come to dinner at my place to celebrate her birthday. I said I would cook and we set the date for two weeks ahead. On the scheduled day, I baked her favorite cake. I cooked other foods I knew she enjoyed. One hour before she was to arrive, I received her call. She wasn't coming to dinner. There wasn't any emergency; she just "didn't feel up to it." I felt hurt and told her so. After one too many broken promises, she lost my respect. We no longer spend time together.

Authenticity

Be yourself. It will not work to try to be someone else. Young people, especially, are affected by peer pressure and always have been, but this is certainly not limited to teenagers. The challenge of authenticity can show up in us in the form of addictions, unhealthy competing, and overspending. It is a waste of time and energy to be a people pleaser. Run your own race. Do not copy anyone else. Be the original that you are. Be the Truth of who you are.

The Truth is that your Soul is authentic. It cannot be otherwise because it is a part of the One Soul...of God's Soul. Our Soul has chosen this lifetime to heal, change, and grow out of what may have been blockages on its long journey. Choosing to do things differently, and with more awareness, our Soul continues to seek enlightenment and the One consciousness. Our Soul is not separate from us, it IS us. While we are in this physical body, on this planet of dense energy, we get lost in the negativity and ego-based mentality of the world which wants us to be like everyone else. There is pressure to be a size zero and to drive a certain type of car. BE the authentic YOU. You are unique. Celebrate your uniqueness by just being yourself.

Your Inner Spark

You inner spark is your authentic self...your Soul. When we identify our Soul, we realize the possibility of connecting to the bigger energy. We may choose to begin the search and possible connection to something greater by stepping onto a spiritual path. This is the Soul's desire to be in alignment once again with its Creator. Remember, the Soul is authentic and wants to live mindfully and consciously as its True-Self.

Open your journal and begin writing about your authentic self. Give yourself credit for your acts of integrity, authenticity, and self respect. Where have you been inauthentic and out of integrity? What do you feel you still need to work on in this area?

Accountability

The Merriam Webster dictionary (2005) defines accountability as: *the quality or state of being accountable; especially an obligation or willingness to accept responsibility or to account for one's actions.*

Who are you accountable to? Maybe a boss, your spouse, your children, your parents, your teachers, your community, or the government? What about to yourself? Being accountable in your life gives you the opportunity to earn respect and trust from others.

What are you responsible for? Are you accountable and do you live up to your responsibilities? If you are not accountable and do not meet your responsibilities, don't expect to receive trust and respect.

Remember we all have choices as to how we create our experiences in this world.

What is important to you?

Affirmational Prayer

As I rest in the Allness of the Holy One, I am embraced in undeniable loving kindness. I live in the Truth of the

Universal Principles, and, as I practice my centeredness, I am filled with joy and peace.

A rich abundance of Good flows to me, beyond my initial expectations of God's blessings.

I choose to walk an ethical path of integrity, honesty, authenticity, accountability, and Truth. I fear no evil, because I know that my God knows of no evil. It only knows of love and light.

The benevolent, Divine Intelligence always knows what I need and want, according to what I think, say, and feel. I create from knowing this Truth. I walk and talk the path of right thinking and right action.

In full thanksgiving, I send this prayer into the Universal energy that always says, "Yes" to me. It is now received here in my experience.

And in gratitude I say, And So It Is!

Amen, Shanti, Shanti, Shanti.

~ Part 3 ~
Create Connection

IN-SIGHTEDNESS

Intuition

Almost everyone is born with five senses. Our five sensory experiences are defined as a one sensory system known as physical reality.

But five senses are no longer enough. The world is changing quickly and continuously. We need to be multi-sensory. My definition of multi-sensory is that in addition to (not instead of) our five senses of hearing, seeing, tasting, smelling, and touching, we would benefit from using the additional senses available to us. I am referring to clairvoyance (clear mental vision), clairaudience (clear hearing at the spiritual level), clairsentience (clear sensing and feeling), and prophetic knowing (absolute certainty). Being multi-sensory extends beyond the physical. When we are multi-sensory, we are more aware. We operate from the power of intuition. Two of our great master teachers, Jesus and the Buddha, were multi-sensory Beings in a physical form. Their heightened levels of spiritual connection and heightened awareness and consciousness have awakened within us the recognition of the cosmic Truths.[25]

Intuition, which I like to call In-sightedness, is how we connect with our spiritual inner knowing of Truths as provided by the Universal One Mind. Yes, everyone has intuition, but not everyone uses it. If you are only focused on the exterior, the outside of self—materialism, vanity, and the illusions of this world—you miss the true essence of life. The inner-life is the connection to the All-ness and Oneness of the personal spiritual experience.

If you have not yet developed your multi-sensory abilities, it's never too late to learn. Begin by exploring programs and teachings of this system in your local area. It will offer you another dimension of personal and spiritual growth.

Cosmic Reality

The reality is that our physical reality is the illusion. Planet earth has very dense energy, not only from the pull of gravity, but also from the deep negativity of fear that can be both overt and covert. In this density, humans walk around in a sort of trance that is dominated by the egoic mind. In its unconscious state, the negative, collective subconscious continues to perpetrate fear, hate, anger, and ignorance that do not serve the whole of humankind. Your mind

---

25 *Universal Cosmic Law, The Seven Principles*, http://www.pymander.com/AETHEREAL/PRINC~1.htm

and feelings are influenced by advertising, news media, television, and radio programming.

In our collective minds even our neighbors and our community influence us. If you feel stressed and worried and are having negative thoughts, take a moment to ask yourself, *Is this my thinking or is it someone else's thinking?* When you are aware of this reality, you have the choice to consciously correct your thinking. Release the negative thought and replace it with gratitude or whatever positive thought you desire. Once you integrate the knowing that *what we focus our attention on is what we create in our "reality,"* you will be operating from a place of personal power.

In the beginning of this book, I wrote about the difference between the Soul ego-mind with a personality of Light versus its opposite, the negative, dark, human, egoic-mind personality. Our Soul holds a different level of thinking and works to transform our human-personality so that we can reach enlightenment. By recognizing your Soul and following its guidance to Source, you will find the peace you are seeking.

In the Universal consciousness, there is only love. There is only One Mind in the whole galaxy. Our Souls continually want to move into the All-ness of the love that this One Mind holds. It is imperative that we learn to love. All is consciousness and All is connected. Every thought we have ripples out into the Cosmos and affects All.

We share the same One Mind. When we begin to understand how influential our thoughts are, we can take responsibility for what we contribute to the Whole.

One of the Four Buddhist Vows is *"I seek my own enlightenment for the purpose of helping all others."*[26] Yes, as we first help ourselves, we then help the collective Universal Soul.

In the spiritual thought community, the year 2012 was called the Time of Awakening. I believe that our intuitive center, the sixth chakra (the pineal gland), also known as our *seat of awareness,* is more fully awakening to our oneness, our spiritual connection, our energy, and to our need to change which enables us to feel in alignment with love. Our awakening is a continuum. I recommend *The Source Field Investigations* by David Wilcock as another useful source of information on this subject.

Take a moment to document in your journal any awareness that may be surfacing for you, your thoughts pertaining to this subject, and if you feel or witness the possibility that you are intuitively picking up others' thoughts and feelings.

Cosmic Evolution

Our world and its people are rapidly developing a stronger and deeper level of awareness. The planetary system, including earth, is experiencing major shifts that not only create environmental change but also physical, emotional, and spiritual changes to human beings. Do

26 *The Basic Teachings of Buddha* ("Following the Buddha's Footsteps," online course, San Francisco State University, n.d.). online.sfsu.edu/rone/Buddhism/footsteps.htm

you feel time propelling you forward faster than ever? Do you sometimes feel disoriented? Do you feel physical or emotional aches and pains beyond your normal experience?

During the latter half of 2012 and the first half of 2013, our planet and the solar system experienced powerful energy shifts via multiple lunar and solar eclipses and solar flares, which then affected human beings. During a solar eclipse, the earth's energy field intensifies and we feel energy more strongly. Our nervous systems are affected. We may feel stronger negative and positive reactions to everything. We may feel anxious, unsettled, nervous, frustrated, inner unrest, even depressed. On the other hand, we may be more in touch with our compassion, inner peace, joy, and have a sense of excitement about "something new" coming. There is no right or wrong way to experience energy. Not everyone understands what is creating their experiences. However, more and more people are witnessing something "different."

In October of 2012, the Global Coherence Initiative[27] reported that *solar flares seem to be related to negative and positive emotional peaks in humans. Bursts of creativity and scientific and societal progress have been linked to the increased energy influx from solar flares. Just as the sun can change water, it is possible that the increased energy from solar flares may help people purge the old and experience positive changes.*

---

27   http://www.glcoherence.org/monitoring-system/commentaries. html

When the negative egoic energy has not been identified within oneself and is not STOPPED, you may have a stronger experience of negativity than ever before. Energy is energy, which is now being amplified. The lies, secrets, and deceptions, which you may have attempted to bury, ignore, deny, and cover up will begin surfacing at this time. They will come back to haunt you so you have to face your past choices. Look around you and within our world. More and more lies and secrets are rising to awareness within families, relationships, communities, governments, and world issues. I believe that this shift in consciousness and awareness has been behind the world-wide revolutions. People have had enough deception—egoic energy. It is time to move into the awareness and consciousness of the Light mentality.

Whatever new awareness you may be having, pay attention, stay centered, be calm, listen more, think before you speak, have compassion for yourself and others, and most importantly stay in your heart center of love.

As we awaken, our human intention is to live a life of purpose, to hold a mentality of service to others, and to operate from a place of loving-kindness. I suggest that your personal growth during this time of major evolution may need to be supplemented by education, experiential learning, and a support system.

For more information on solar and lunar eclipses and solar flares, see these two websites: http://spaceweather.com and http://csep10.phys.UTK.edu/astr161/lect/time/eclipses.html

How fast should you grow? That is your decision. There is no right or wrong way to grow. I don't care how fast you grow. God does not care how fast you grow. Only your Soul knows its own desire for growth. Honor yourself and know that you are doing the very best you know how to do in your current level of consciousness.

The teachings of the wise ones strongly suggest we have a willingness to move into a higher level of consciousness along a path toward enlightenment. Siddhartha Gautama, the Buddha, taught that it is possible to achieve enlightenment within one lifetime. That is a powerful teaching, is it not? Even though the Buddha claimed that suffering is the experience of life, I believe that when we focus, hold an intention, and practice identifying and eliminating the thought that we must stay in pain and suffering, we can live with a different perception. Buddhism teaches the necessity of meditation, a centering practice of stillness, silence, and allowing the flow of inner awareness to develop. Find your center of peace and enter your path toward enlightenment.

During this evolutionary time, forgiveness of self and, therefore, of all others is extremely important. You may want to review Chapter 6, "Forgiveness."

Allowing yourself to move into full awareness of how God created you to live and be, along with loving and accepting yourself unconditionally would be the greatest gift you could ever receive from yourself. As Joseph Campbell wrote, *"The privilege of a lifetime is being who you are."*[28]

---

28   Joseph Campbell, *Reflections on the Art of Living: A Joseph Campbell Companion* (New York: HarperCollins, 1991).

Take this opportunity to write in your journal regarding your true feelings about what you witness in the world and yourself. Where do you feel connection? Where, and with what, are you disconnected? With whom are you disconnected? List all the ways you feel lost and alone. Answer these questions. Do you want more awareness in your life? What are you now willing to do to bring change into your life?

Is Ignorance Bliss?

It is said that "ignorance is bliss." Sometimes I try to remember back to being unaware and in a blissful place, but I really do not believe that ignorance and bliss go together. When I was unaware, unconscious, and insensitive to others, I was not a loving or happy person. Neither were the friends I had at that time, but I didn't see it then. One of my dearest friends had a sharp wit with a cutting sense of humor. I loved being with him and thought he was clever. We laughed a lot. Looking back at our jokes and cutting comments, however, I realize now that I laughed with him at other people's expense. I am not proud of my old critical, judgmental self.

It took me awhile to awaken, heal my insensitivity, and learn compassion. The day I realized I had changed and had moved into a higher level of consciousness and compassion was a day I will never forget. I was at a wonderful spiritual social event with several friends in my "spiritual circle." I was sitting near two of them, waiting for drummers to perform, when I overheard my companions laughing. I certainly didn't want to miss the fun, so I asked them what they were laughing about. One of them said, "We're looking at the "pig family," and they both pointed at a mother and her two children. I thought the mother and her kids were cute, with their turned up noses. I was appalled at the slur and felt a pain in my heart center. I said, "How can you be so cruel! That was a terrible thing to say." My two friends just snarled at me and said, "Oh, lighten up, Judy!"

At that moment, I knew I was spending time with the wrong people. I knew I had evolved into consciousness and compassion, but these people hadn't evolved yet. That doesn't mean they were right or wrong, but it was time for me to move on. I had reached a new level of awareness. Humor is crucial in life, but not at another person's expense.

Through the years, as I have chosen to strongly focus on my spiritual growth and level of consciousness and compassion, many people have come and many people have gone in my life. Sometimes I move on, sometimes they move on.

DIANE

After three decades of being close friends and confidants, something changed. Diane and I had seen each other through weddings, marriages, divorces, births, deaths, illnesses, child-birthing and child-rearing, careers, relocations, change, struggles, and many joys. We promised each other that we would never leave the other, when so many people had left us. We called ourselves Soul Sisters.

I was heartbroken when I realized that Diane had broken ties with me. No matter where we had lived in the world, for thirty years, we always maintained connection. But the day came, after sending Diane numerous messages through every medium I had available, asking her to please respond, to please share any issue she had with me, to please tell me what had I done wrong; I went to dread. I went to the assumption that I was not good enough, or something was wrong with me. I was hurt deeply. After a period of denial, I realized I would not be hearing back from her. The saddest part for me was that Diane could not tell me why she chose to leave. After a lot of processing, I have become aware that with each personal growth step I take, people fall away from me. I believe that as we release dysfunctional thinking and behavior, it is nearly impossible to maintain a friendship with a person who still lives in egoic-dysfunction. Neither one of us will be comfortable.

This is not the first story I've shared with you that has this theme, is it? I trust in the Higher Power and my connection to It. Whatever the deeper message is for why anything happens in our lives is for us to discover. As I grieve my loss, I journal my thoughts, and I pray for strength and know that as we all move on in our lives, everything is for our highest good. I send my old friend love and light energy of peace.

It's important to monitor the types of people in your circle of influence. The Buddha called this "Right Association." Right Association is the preliminary step to the Eightfold Path often mentioned by the Buddha. Training for a life with spirit is made less arduous if you can be with others who seek the same things. Of course, it's hard to leave unenlightened people you love, but there comes a time when you must allow yourself to move into a higher level of vibration. I have chosen to release those people from my life because they do not reflect who or where I want to be.

Take a moment to write in your journal any similar experiences you may have had in your life. List the names of the people who may have left you and the names of the people you may have left. Think about the reasons why and write them down as well. Now move into forgiveness, again.

Family Awareness

Your family may be a big challenge to you. They may not be where you want them to be or who you think they "should" be. In your perception, they may not be aware or connected. Do you judge your family? Even if we are physically or emotionally separated from them, we still have a genetic and Soul connection.

Science is in the early stages of discovering what they call "emotional inheritance," which I prefer to call emotional genetics. According to the Laboratory of Neurogenetics, in a very interesting review titled "Genetics of Emotions," it is written that *Emotionality is 40-60 percent inheritable....*[29]

I believe that we are genetically affected by multiple generations of ancestors at the emotional level as well as the physical level. We now understand that we can inherit family diseases such as heart disease and diabetes. It's in the genes! Our connection with the family allows us to learn more about ourselves. We all have an opportunity to change that which is within us. In my experience as an intuitive spiritual healer working with emotional and physical genetics, I have witnessed multiple amazing healings by our Creator. Many stories and examples of these healings can be found on my website: http://www.themysteryschool.org. Please see the pages titled *Success Stories* and *Testimonials*.

You have a choice. Choose change and the healing you need so you can move forward into the development of higher consciousness, greater awareness, and health. You are at a fork in the road every moment of your life. How do you decide what your next step will be? How do you perceive your world? When you take responsibility for your feelings and events that appear to be challenges and decide to move into change, you will feel powerful.

What decisions are you trying to make at the present time? Are you at a crossroads? Do you know someone who is trying to block your growth? Are you blocking your own growth? Remember that *you are powerful*. In your journal,

---

29   Laura Bevilacqua and David Goldman, *Trends in Cognitive Sciences, Genetics of Emotions* (Rockville, MD: Cell Press, Laboratory of Neurogenetics, National Institution of Alcohol Abuse and Alcoholism), Sept. 2011, Vol.15, No.9.

list the ways you feel your power and the ways you feel powerless.

Who Am I?

You are your Soul. You are the light of the Cosmos created in human form. You are one with the Universe. You are a divine expression of God-consciousness. When you remember that you are one with God, the healing begins.

I believe God is good. God reflects health, wealth, and happiness. If you do not have these gifts in your life, you may be wishing you did. Our thoughts, feelings, and words create our actions, which create the results in our outer reality and what we perceive as our reality. Lack is not God's Truth. The belief in lack is the fearful ego mind that wants to keep you "safe" right where you are. But you may be in illness, debt, worry, depression, anxiety, fear, stress, disease, and unhealthy relationships. These are appearances... not Truth.

How do we create a different reality? How do we move into and live in the energy of healing? Our minds are powerful. Our thoughts are powerful. Make a decision this very moment to stop believing that your thoughts are the truth of who you are. *You are not your thoughts.*

On Being Human's fascinating website, http://www.beinghuman.org, it is written:

For most of human history we've been trying to understand our lives based on metaphysical, religious, and supernatural concepts. Then the Age of

Enlightenment ushered in science and Darwin's remarkable theory of evolution—a powerful new way to look at ourselves and the world. Now disciplines such as cognitive neuroscience, evolutionary psychology, genetics, anthropology, and philosophy are delivering fascinating new findings which have the potential to radically remake the way we see ourselves. Based on these scientific insights, a more comprehensive view of human nature is now emerging.

In the quest to gain a clearer view of human nature, we at Being Human have sought out the people who have made a unique contribution to the growing understanding of our species. Neuroscientists, psychologists, philosophers, primatologists, and more; we feature these brilliant minds, who we call Luminaries.

You are God-consciousness in human form. Let this Truth shine. Become aware of the negative thoughts that want to hold you back, and want to keep you from changing. Negative thinking creates negative energy in every part of our body. Our body talks to us through dis-order, disease, and illness. This is how our body lets us know we are in wrong thinking. Every disorder has a metaphysical meaning. I suggest that you read Louise Hay's book, *Heal Your Body*, as a source of metaphysical interpretations of disease.

Change your thoughts, change your feelings, change your actions, and change the words you speak. When you allow healing through change, the trajectory of your life path will never be the same.

We know what we fear in our conscious mind, but do we know what we fear subconsciously? Probably not. Our subconscious mind is stronger and may carry deep fears created through past experiences.

Neuroscientist Richard Davidson has spent nearly forty years studying the human brain and emotions. The conclusion he's reached after all that research? He writes, *With some effort, you can change the brain circuits governing your emotions and shape your emotional style.* Davidson and other researchers continue to find evidence that the brain is incredibly plastic, and that many things we think are hardwired into us, aren't set in stone. By understanding our emotions, how they arise, and where they come from, we can become more aware of our own emotional styles. With that awareness, we can shape our responses to make our lives better, changing our brains one bit at a time.

What are your fears? Think about this. How did your primary caretakers demonstrate life to you? What were their beliefs about health? Did they tell you or act out their fears? Any fear that pops into your mind is the egoic thought process that you think is the truth of you. It's time to allow healing to begin within you. When you allow your spiritual self to heal—your thoughts, your inner child, emotions, feelings, and physical body will begin to catch up—and you will move into a healing pattern of wholeness. This is God's way. This is the Universal Holy One's intention.

I suggest that including a wellness program of nutritional guidance and naturopathic advice, where needed, can also be part of your journey to health. At different times on my personal journey, I have incorporated the following holistic modalities: acupuncture, iridology, Healing Touch, Reiki, P.U.S.H., (a hands-on healing modality), cranial sacral, deep tissue massage, reflexology, Chinese herbs, health supplements, spiritual counseling, Atlas Chiropractic and Network Chiropractic, yoga, and meditation, to name a few. I have been gluten-free since February 2013.

When you explore the idea of change, you may have feelings of discomfort. Take some time now to write in your journal about what is coming up for you. What do you want to release? How is your health? What are the genetic diseases in your family history? Are you willing to explore alternative health care? Take your time and be kind to yourself as you journal and discover more about who you are. This is your journey, no one else's.

What Would J.B. Ange Do?

This question was printed on a bumper sticker, along with J.B.'s image, after his death.

In 2000, when I moved to the small town in northern Colorado where I live, I often noticed a man riding a bicycle around town with a large black trash bag attached to the handlebars. This was J.B. Ange. He was collecting trash from the side of the road and waving to passers-by with a big smile on his face. No matter the season, he could always be seen on that bike. I didn't know who he was, but I assumed he was homeless.

As years went by, I often saw J.B. around town. He waved and smiled at me as if he knew me. I never asked anyone who he was, and I never heard anyone speak of him…until the day in 2009 when he was riding his bicycle along a major road and was hit by a car and killed instantly. When the news of Mr. Ange's tragic death hit our town, everyone began sharing their personal experience with this loving, kind, and giving Soul.

J.B. was not homeless. He lived in town with his brother and sister-in-law. He gathered recyclables to earn some money to help others. The stories began flooding the town about how he was always smiling as he positioned himself at a grocery store door to hold it open for customers, always greeting them.

Then there was the story that J.B. had heard of a single mother with two little children. When one of the children's tricycle broke, he quietly took it to be repaired and surprised the child and her mother, asking nothing in return. He bought coffee for the store's employees on a cold winter morning just to help them warm up. One of the recipients of his good deeds shared that she often bought him coffee, too, which he graciously received. He was making friends all over town, though no one really knew him.

Our little town deeply grieved his passing. It was reported in the local paper that there were more than two thousand people at his memorial service, including members of the police department, the fire department, and the town's mayor. The largest church in town held his memorial service and was overflowing. The newspaper article about Mr. Ange was two full pages long.

A year later, a full-sized statue of J.B. Ange was erected in the center of the town plaza. It was fully paid for by contributions of those who loved him. Almost everyone had the bumper sticker on the back of their car that said, "What would J.B. Ange do?"

Why am I sharing this story? Because all these years later we here in J.B.'s town are still talking about him and how he selflessly gave to others. His soul purpose was actuated.

I recently spent an evening with my son and his wife and for some reason J.B.'s name came up. We shared our memories. My daughter-in-heart said, "I wonder why he had to die when he did." My son, in his Soul's knowing, said, "He had to die then because people had to wake up to the unconditional love, kindness, generosity, and heart he brought to the world. Here we are today, so many years after his passing, and we are still talking and learning more from him. I think he was a demonstration of good that needed to be seen at this time."

I completely agree. J.B. gave his community another way to see love right in front of them. He served the only way he knew how…by giving love, respect, attention, and appreciation to his fellow human beings. He died doing what he loved. His life was not wasted. He has left an imprint on our Souls, one wave and a smile at a time. He blessed our lives with his presence.

What kind of legacy will you leave?

What Are You Called to Do?

All our paths are different, of course. Whatever your purpose or passion may be, move forward fully into it. Then you will begin to feel complete, whole, and healthy. People often ask what their purpose is in this lifetime.

What do you love to do? What do you feel your talents are, where do you feel you shine? This is where you will find your life's purpose. Your purpose is not complicated or hidden from you. God would not do that to you. Your talents are not a secret unless you decide to keep them secret.

Is the negative ego telling you, once again, that you are not good enough and that your gifts are not enough? Okay, then study, learn, practice, and practice more that which you feel pulled to do. Stepping out of your comfort zone may be exactly what you need to do to discover what lies deep within your abilities.

I cannot carry a tune in a bucket, but I have written poetry. Once the poem has come out of my mind and been written down, another energy is created through the Universe. Little did I know, many years ago, that a poem I heard in my head and then wrote down on paper became lyrics for a theme song for my community television program, which was called *Healing Voices*.

Please bear with me here as I share a couple of personal experiences of self discovery. Back in the mid-90s, I was invited to be a guest on a California community television program to discuss my work as a medical intuitive. As I was watching the camera crew, production, and the host of the program, I had a thought that it looked like fun to host a program. I remember thinking, "I could do this." Later I contacted the television station, asked questions, presented my program concept, took training, and became the producer and host of my own community television program, *Healing Voices*, which I produced and hosted for four years.

It is said that the Universe is always conspiring to help us create that which we believe. After writing the *Healing Voices* poem/lyrics, I could hear the music in my head that was meant to be behind the lyrics. One day I was interviewing a musical group and a vocalist on my program. While they were performing, I had a thought to ask the leader if she would be interested in creating the music to go with my lyrics. Their flutiest was available and interested in being the creative music force. I didn't have the funds for such an endeavor, but she was willing to be a part of the process for credits and copyright for her music. Within two months, I received a package in my mailbox that contained a cassette tape of my theme song with beautiful Native American flute music and a professional vocalist who had also volunteered to be a part of the creative process. From that day forward, my TV program had its theme song playing at the beginning and end of each show with the credits running for the contributors. It was all a work of love, divinely orchestrated by the Universe. Did I make money from my program during those four years? No, not directly. But in addition to serving my community, new clients came to my practice for my services. We are always taken care of by the Universe. We only need to open our eyes, our hearts, and our minds to how that may happen.

Open your journal again and begin listing everything you love to do. What makes your heart sing? What makes you smile? What is your dream? Be creative and open your mind to new ideas. Let the creative Universe in and write down what comes into your heart. Now list all the doubts and fears you have regarding your dreams. Then tear them up or scratch them out of your journal. The doubts and fears are a waste of time.

We never know what we are capable of until we try. Follow your Soul's lead. When I had the thought, the idea, of having my own community television program, I had a choice. I could listen to the ego that says, "Are you kidding me? You don't know anything about producing, hosting, recruiting guests, running cameras, editing, set decorating, or sound. Who do you think you are?" Or I could do what I did, for the period of time the Universe wanted me to serve the local community by bringing forward metaphysical education, spiritual information, and an opportunity for guests to be heard and seen, so others could learn and receive.

Take a risk. Learn something new. Don't get stuck in the can't dos. Take a chance. If whatever that is doesn't work out...*so what*? Do something else. We are not meant to stagnate in the same place forever. These are simply steps on your growth path. You can do anything you put your mind to. As I learned something new, I was helping others and having fun at the same time. So can you.

Do You Feel Called to Be a Healer?

Let us now address the concept of being a healer as a profession. Let me preface my words by saying that none of *us* are the healers. *God is the Healer.* Jesus said, "It is not I, but the Father within that doeth the work" (John 14:10).

We who serve by being the conduit for Source's work call ourselves healers. A definition of "metaphysics" is, *the branch of philosophy that deals with the first principles of things, including abstract concepts such as being, knowing, substance, cause, identity, time, and space.*[30] I often define metaphysics as that which is beyond the body.

I am proud to say I serve my Source as an interfaith minister, spiritual counselor, medical intuitive healer, and metaphysician. The gifts of a healer are sacred. We have chosen to come into this lifetime to serve others in this particular way. I believe that some people have chosen to move into the traditional medical profession instead of one of the alternative healing professions, out of a subconscious fear of being ridiculed, judged, or ostracized by their church, society, families, or friends. This is common when their past lives may have been full of pain and torture for being "different." Perhaps in a past life such a healer was persecuted by the Inquisition.

In earlier times, the healer was the midwife, the

---

30   *Merriam-Webster's Dictionary,* 2005.

herbalist, the medicine man or woman, or the wise woman of the town who helped the ill and diseased survive and heal. Such healers often lived in rural areas and were the "go-to" people when the members of their community were in physical peril. Through the centuries, however, these healers were ridiculed, judged, threatened, and even killed.

I suggest an informative and educational book pertaining to this very issue, called *Women Healers: Portraits of Herbalists, Physicians, and Midwives*. The book focuses on women because of their gender majority in this field. The author writes in her conclusion that "this book has moved through time from the very distant pre-patriarchal past to the present day. From a world where a woman as a healer was the norm to a time where women have to fight even to ensure that gentle, holistic methods of treatment have a voice alongside aggressive mechanistic medical techniques." [31] I am not purposely leaving the male healers from this message, but in my experience of over twenty years of teaching metaphysical energy healing classes, only about ten percent of the attendees are male.

Many of my students and clients have shared with me that they want to be in the healing field, but they are afraid of becoming healers. They're afraid of their intuition and inner knowing. If healing is the profession you feel called to, I suggest you seek reputable, professional training from an ethical, highly recommended, metaphysical teacher to

---

31 Elisabeth Brooke, *Women Healers: Portraits of Herbalists, Physicians, and Midwives* (Rochester, VT: Healing Arts Press, 1995), p. 149.

become the best practitioner of "healing modalities" that you can be. If the medical profession is calling to you, then by all means, seek the best medical training available.

Through the years I have had many practicing medical doctors and nurses, along with various medical professionals, attend my classes in medical intuition and DNA and genetic healing techniques. I am grateful to teach alternative methods to these professionals who have told me that they *want to move beyond the limitations of their medical training, which cures, but does not heal*, and incorporate holistic healing methods into their work.

Receiving Guidance

I believe we will not have clarity on our Soul's purpose until we have learned the skills that will support us in whatever that role will be. That does not mean we need to know everything right away. It means we need to begin building the foundation for our life's purpose. When I spent several decades in corporate America learning sales, marketing, training modalities, public relations, management, communication, and even producing and hosting a TV program, I didn't know what my life's purpose was meant to be. But what I learned created a foundation for the business I later started and the private practice in which I now serve.

I had a life-changing health crisis in the late 1980s that shifted me out of corporate America and into the healing arts. For over a year, I thought I was in early menopause (I was only forty-two). I had many symptoms. I had the dreaded hot flashes, night sweats, mood swings, memory loss, very low energy, and weight gain. As I attempted to get through the challenging life change on my own, eventually my symptoms were so severe I decided to visit my gynecologist for hormone therapy. After the checkup and a blood draw, I received a call the next day from the doctor's office to tell me I needed to visit an endocrinologist immediately. They didn't explain why, only that I was in *a state of emergency*. They referred me to an endocrinologist who would take my appointment right away.

After many tests were run, I was diagnosed with hypothyroidism and I was told that my thyroid was ninety-five percent dead. We cannot live without our thyroid or thyroid replacement therapy, if our thyroid is challenged. The doctor immediately placed me on a medication. First, a low dose, and during a nine month period and numerous visits, the medication was slowly adjusted to the therapeutic amount for me. But during this entire time, my symptoms increased. I was miserable. I felt like I was getting worse.

My health was so challenged that I was unable to work. At that time in my life I was a realtor with a large firm. I was on commission, which meant that if I couldn't work, then I didn't make any money. The stress of not making money and my inability to pay my bills added to my health crisis.

After nine months of treatment, the endocrinologist sent me back to my gynecologist because he said I was also in early menopause. I said, "I told you so." The doctor explained to me that the symptoms of hypothyroidism and menopause are very similar. He added that the hypothyroidism had to be controlled first. Otherwise, I would die, but I would not die from menopause. Very funny...I wouldn't die from menopause...I just wanted to.

I wanted relief. I wanted to feel like my old self. I wanted hormone therapy immediately! So, I got it, but I have never felt like my old self again. My body would never be the same. It took another two years for me to even begin to feel somewhat like my original, energetic self.

After such a long time from the real estate business and my inability to handle that level of stress again, I was then drawn to a completely different way of thinking and Being. I was changing and becoming aware that everything in my life had to change. Source began to show me a new direction for my life's journey.

When I found myself on a very different path, I came alive. This was the point in my life when I began my studies in hypnotherapy and began a private practice. I was excited, stimulated, and knew that I had found my calling. I then began learning new skills, not to replace the old ones, but to create more tools to help others. Reiki (pronounced *ray-key*) was an additional tool that I studied, became attuned to, and added to my skill "toolbox". In 1994, I became a Reiki Master/Teacher. For many years I not only used the power of Reiki on clients, but also taught this powerful method of healing to students.

At that time in my life I was slowly becoming aware of the difference between religion and spirituality. I had a challenge saying the word "God," let alone attending any traditional church. I was pushed, and more often pulled, to seek the healing my Soul needed. I felt led to step onto a spiritual path, and I began the lifelong journey that has brought me to celebrations of many spiritual paths. For me, I see spirituality as an "inner" growth experience and religion as an experience of separatism. I wanted to find my truth.

In my search all those years ago I found, then chose to study, participate in, and eventually teach the Goddess traditions. I became involved in Wicca and became an elder in a Dianic (women only) Wiccan circle. We honored various goddesses and their holy days. It was a wonderful time of spiritual growth for me.

A few years later I was introduced to Gnosticism. Once I studied it, I was pleased to learn that Gnosticism embraced the male/female paradigm. I was beginning to heal my "God" issues and I joined the Gnostic church. It felt balanced to me, and I realized that I needed to move into spiritual balance. At that time, I also began studying shamanism and attended services at local Native American gatherings. Toward the end of the 1990s, I discovered Religious Science, or Science of Mind, which is very interfaith-based. Unity is similar and another New Thought philosophy I attended, however the teachings of Religious Science make up the philosophy that is the solid foundation of my current teachings and writings.

As I studied and practiced many sacred traditions I was finding myself and my Soul center. I was discovering what felt right to me and what called to me. A lot of negativity was released as I learned how to stay in the light more times than not. My spiritual journey has been a long one. There is no right or wrong for any of us, as to how long we are on the journey. I plan to be on it the rest of this lifetime and many lifetimes to come.

Throughout my journey I have learned that everything in my life is divinely orchestrated. In 1999 I was spiritually led to begin training in DNA and genetic healing processes. After approximately a year of studies and practice I took teachers training so I could provide this system to my students. The techniques are very user-friendly, so I used what I had learned on myself and my life changed even more. I was clearing my belief systems through using this method, when nothing else I tried before would ever clear the deep genetic dysfunctional energy I was carrying. I found my relationships with all my family members shifted into peace and harmony. My level of abundance, in all forms, healed. I was becoming more and more aware of my spiritual connection to the Oneness energy of the Universe. I was personally healing, forgiving, and creating from a new place within my Soul.

From that time on, into the next several years, I discovered that many of my friends saw a difference in me. Many were asking me, "Have you ever thought of becoming a minister?" or telling me, "Judy, you should become a minister." I would laugh and immediately say, "No, I already have a business, I don't need another one." But God had plans for me and was speaking through my friends, trying to get my attention about another part of my journey IT had in mind for me. Inner messages from Source regarding my ministry also began. I was led to ask my ministerial friends about seminaries and methods of study.

I don't exactly remember when I finally said "yes" to God, but I finally did. I said, *Okay, God, if You want me to serve as a minister in addition to what I am doing, then it is up to You to make it happen. I don't know the way, the how, or where the money will come from, but You do. Show me the way.* In early 2009, I overheard a fellow Science of Mind student mention a seminary by name. I had a feeling in my body that was familiar to me when God wants me to pay attention to something that is meaningful to my next step. I asked the student for the website information on The New Seminary she was speaking about. That evening, when I looked it up on the Internet, I could feel the affirmative energy all through my body that this was the "place."

After applying, interviewing, and being accepted, with a scholarship due to all my years in spiritual studies and teachings, I began the 2009-2011 program. I enrolled in The New Seminary for Interfaith Studies in New York City (Manhattan),[32] and my life would never be the same again.

The New Seminary's motto is "Never Instead Of, Always In Addition To." Their motto alone was an indicator to me that I was meant to be in this seminary, because I thought and taught from this same belief.

My spiritual journey has always been very eclectic, so this two year interfaith ministerial program was a beautiful

---

32   The New Seminary for Interfaith Studies, http://www.new-seminary.com/

fit for me. "Honoring All Life-Affirming Paths" is the essence of interfaith.

The focus of our first year was on the study of world religions and sacred texts. Not only would we study and write lengthy papers on the major traditions, but we were also required to make "site visits." This meant visiting local temples, synagogues, churches, centers, and fellowships during their services, In our first year, we also had teleconference study groups, support groups, and deans that were assigned to us and met with on a regular basis.. Because I live in Colorado and the seminary is in New York, they shipped CDs, manuals, and materials for the classes to me on a monthly basis. Two times each year we were required to attend a week of seminary classes at a gorgeous spiritual retreat in upper New York. What a wonderful opportunity that was to meet the directors and deans and spend a lot of time with my fellow seminarians, who were from around the world.

In the second year at the seminary, the focus was on learning, writing, and creating sacred ceremonies, such as weddings, funeral, memorials, and baby blessings and christenings for all faiths. We were required to write several worship services to be performed individually and with a worship team.

Being a minister is not a solitary endeavor. Learning to work with teams, in groups, and collaborating for the good of the whole, is crucial to becoming a great minister. Not only does a minister lead a congregation, but he or she also needs to interact with the board of directors, volunteers, and guest speakers, as well as students when teaching spiritual classes.

Many books were required reading. If you are interested in the names of these sacred texts, I suggest you visit The New Seminary's website for the list.

The seminary journey was a huge growth experience for me. I see the importance of personal growth for all people interested in leading others, as a representative of the Holy One. We cannot take someone else down a path we haven't walked.

I was ordained in June 2011, with my class, in the magnificent Riverside Church in New York City.[33] This cathedral is gorgeous. As of this writing, it has celebrated eighty-three years of providing services to its community. Dr. Martin Luther King and Nelson Mandela both have spoken from the pulpit of Riverside Church. The link given in the footnote takes you to the exquisite art and architecture of this famous site.

How Do I Know I'm on the Divine Path?

You will know you are on the divine path when everything falls into place with ease and grace. With God, there is no struggle. When we turn all fears and doubts over to our Source—with sincere belief and trust that God has our back and all will be handled—we are in grace, we are allowing the natural flow of the Universe to support us, we can breathe, and we have truly released our fears. When we believe,

---

33   http://www.theriversidechurchny.org/about/?art

without doubt, that we always have God's assistance, we always have it.

Unfortunately, many humans are attached to their egoic thoughts and do not really hear guidance. Do you hear the "shoulds" that the egoic mind tells you? Do you think the "shoulds" are the Truth? Typically, "should" is just the ego's opinion. God does not tell us what we should or should not do. Divine guidance will always feel right. Egoic guidance will always feel "off" in some way.

The importance of clear thinking, awareness, and consciousness in spiritual connection needs to be emphasized. Build a relationship with the All-Knowing Divine Intelligence. Your little consciousness, with only five (or six) senses, is very limited. Instead of focusing on your ego connection, focus on developing your intuitive connection through divine guidance. Open yourself to guidance. Whatever you are called to do by your god, you will know it is right because it feels right. God does not call upon us to go to the dark side of negative, evil energy. I repeat: the God I know from all my studies and all my personal experiences of IT is a good God of unconditional love and light.

Trusting God

Not trusting or being afraid to trust, can extend far past our family dynamics. It can extend to not trusting God. Not trusting ourselves. Not trusting the Universe.

Spirituality is very important to me. I believe it should

be important to you. It is where you find the answers to everything. We will not be whole if we are spiritually disconnected. This is not about religious dogma. This is not about organized religion. When we find our god of many names, we find pure love.

If the hairs on the back of your neck stand up when you hear the word spirituality, that tells you this is an area you need to explore. The 14th-century Persian poet Hafiz once said, *"...your separation from God is the hardest work in the world."*

When you connect to your Source, you find peace and joy. It is about finding the god within yourself. It is recognizing a power greater than you that knows everything and can supply you with the answers, along with abundance, health, and happiness.

What Is Prayer?

Prayer is not about calling upon Spirit. True prayer, as I see it, is moving into awareness of Spirit. It is about quieting the mind and listening for answers that will lead us to our highest good.

Spirit does not tell us what to do. Ego tells us what to do. Spirit allows us to move to the fork in the road and make our own choices. As I shared in the story of my personal journey, I have been led to many paths. I could have said *no* at any time to any one of the paths. But I followed my God's lead, because it has always felt right.

Why Doesn't God Answer My Prayers?

We do not get what we pray for; we do not get what we ask for...*we get what we believe*. If, on any level, you believe you are not worthy to receive your good (however you see that to be in your life), then you will not receive your good. Although on the conscious level, we may think we are in alignment with the Universal Good; subconsciously, we may be so unaware of how we create our reality that we continue to live in lack and endure an appearance of suffering. To begin the process of change, we must pay attention to the words we speak and the thoughts we think. From the seed we plant into the rich soil of creation, our experience grows.

Building a relationship with our Source is a powerful experience. Those who choose not to believe in God are still loved by God. In whatever manner we choose to honor him or her, our Source is absolutely fine with that. Remember, God does not care how we worship. Humankind has set up limitations and judgments as to right and wrong. God does not judge right and wrong, good or bad. God just IS.

We do not have to be in a building, a church, a chapel, a synagogue, a center, a temple, a mosque, or any other structure, to give thanks to our Source. It truly is an inside-self job. We can enjoy a powerful experience of God-presence in these environments and with a spiritual leader bringing forth a message from God, but there are countless other ways to experience It.

I experienced God when this poem flowed through me.

There Is Only God

As I stand at the water's edge at sunset, there is God.
As I kneel on a mountaintop at daybreak, there is God.
As I walk a labyrinth in silent meditation, there is God.
As I enjoy a blessed meal with a loved one, there is God.
As I scream in agony while birthing my child, there is God.
As I read, learn, teach, and grow, there is God.
As I share intimacy and unite with my beloved, there is God.
As I receive invasive repair to this physical body, there is God.
As I sit by the bed, holding the hand of a Soul in transition, there is God.
As I look into my son's and grandson's eyes, there is God.
As I laugh, dance, sing, run, and play, there is God.
As I cry out in pain and grief, there is God.
As I create my Soul's vision, there is God.
As I serve humanity and the world, there is God.
As I finish this life's journey and move toward my next Soul journey, there is God.
God is everywhere.
There is no place where God is not.

Since God is not separate from us, but moves through us—as us—we are God in action.

Self-Love

Feeling disconnected from our God-self and God-consciousness leads not only to feeling disconnected from ourselves, but feeling disconnected from others, too.

Disconnection leads to depression, anxiety, frustration, and inappropriate behavior toward our loved ones and humanity as a whole. Spiritual disconnection holds us in the energy of separation. Feeling separated from Source and other people creates fear and imbalance. You may have heard people say that we…"come in alone and we die alone." This is a perfect example of the negative ego talking. The Truth is that God is with us every moment, whether we are conscious of it or not.

Self-love is allowing an inner awareness of God's unconditional love energy to fill us. We can only give what we have. If we do not carry self-love and self-forgiveness, how can we fully love and forgive others?

Self-love is a demonstration of God's love. One way to move into self-love is to express the special gifts God gave you. Along with life itself; we all have one or more talents. Some express their creativity through music, others through cooking, and still others through teaching, designing, engineering, building, healing, painting, writing, acting, singing, or raising animals and/or children.

Affirmational Prayer

If I know nothing else in my life, I know God is love and I am one with God. I am aware of God's love in nature, God's love in all people, all things, and all places.

As I witness God's love, I become an expression of love through my Soul's action. Today and all days, I accept the Truth of love manifest in every area of my life.

I allow my Soul's purpose to reveal Itself to me, in Its time. I embrace my Soul's connection to the Divine, trusting my Divine purpose has been set forth prior to my earthly arrival in this physical form.

I trust that my God and my Soul are leading me onto the path that is my Soul's greatest mission in this lifetime. I release all judgment as to what that mission is and when it will be shown to me.

I inhale trust and exhale worry.

I inhale patience and exhale control.

I inhale love and exhale fear.

I know that where I am in my life is right where I am meant to be in this moment. I am right where I am because this is how I currently serve.

I relax and trust God's leadership. When I am meant to step onto another part of my path, I will say, "Yes." All is Good, All is God, and All is done as it is spoken.

I am in complete gratitude for this knowing, and I release this affirmation into the Universe for manifestation right in this moment.

And so it is, Amen.

WHO IS GOD?

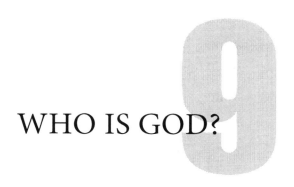

"We are God, in drag."

—Deepak Chopra, *The Rabbit Hole*

A s we study what is known about our universe and the trillions of galaxies in it, we still know so little. What we do know is that we are a microscopic pinpoint, in the whole of existence. We were all created out of the same Big Bang. Evolution brought all of us to where we are today. Because we have an innate knowing of the Truth and connection to the One energy, we may feel overwhelmed and uncomprehending as we learn that we are an important part of the power of the unending galaxy.

To truly know there is so much more to our Soul journey than we can ever imagine, we must be willing to step into the unknown with complete trust that we are safe in our discoveries, if we stay connected to the Light.

I cannot prove it, but I feel that because we have polarities on our planet, we need to think about the endless universes and galaxies as possibly also having polarities.

Just maybe the dichotomy of dark ego and light exists throughout All there is. I wonder if we will discover the answers to these conjectures within our lifetime.

Fear of God

What are your fear-based thoughts about God? Were you once told that you are separate from God? Were you taught that God would judge and punish you, that God would withhold love and abundance from you if you were not a good little boy or girl? Were you told you were not as good as Jesus was? That you could not bring God's healing to others, because only Jesus could do that?

Some traditions believe that Jesus Is God. I agree. I believe that God worked through Jesus and as Jesus. Jesus fully demonstrated God-consciousness into the world. I also believe that *we are God in form*. Remember, we are one with the One (God). Our Soul's mission here on earth is to move up to the level of awareness that Jesus had. We are only held back from moving into—and living in—this consciousness by our own negative thinking and the negative collective consciousness. Do not allow anyone to tell you that you are not as good as Jesus. Do not allow anyone to tell you that you cannot do what Jesus could do. Those that do not believe in themselves and the innate gifts that God gave them and do not believe they are good enough, will attempt to keep others from finding their divinity.

What negative, lie-filled messages have you received? As you think of the messages, list them in your journal and allow yourself to feel your body's response to these messages. Do you feel anxious, angry, tense, fearful, or stressed? How does your body react? Do you feel tightness in your stomach, chest, or throat? Negative reactions in your body represent negative thoughts held in your mind. Wherever you experience negative feelings, fear is there. Even if you are unaware, the Universal Light is right here waiting for you to reconnect to its Truth.

God does not judge, punish, or withhold love and abundance. But we do that to each other and to ourselves. My friend, David Sun Todd,[34] said something to me I've always remembered. He said, *"There is nothing more deadly than the fear of God. Disconnection from God is spiritual death."* Thank you, David.

What Did I Do to Make God Mad?

Absolutely nothing!

Some of us were taught that God is an angry God. Hinduism, which is said to be the world's oldest organizing religion, teaches that there are gods and goddesses that demonstrate all the aspects of energy, including negative ones. I see these deities as representatives of all forms of human thinking.

Who are we angry with? If we are angry with God, I believe we are actually angry with ourselves. Why are we directing it away from ourselves? If we understand that the Universal God is impartial and impersonal, then we cannot

---

34   http://www.bellandtodd.com/

blame or be angry with God for what happens in our life or in our world. I choose to embrace a benevolent God. I do not believe God is an angry God.

It's God's Fault!

Have you blamed God for something that has happened in your life rather than accepting that your Soul chose the experience to help you grow? We blame God for everything—like the death of a loved one, lack, poverty, a disease, environmental disasters, war, and the loss of a job. Even terrorists declare their destructive actions to be "in the name of God." The horrendous things that take place in this world are confusing and dismaying. But it's not God's fault when you, your family, your neighbors, politicians, or the government make bad decisions. It's not God's fault that humans are greedy and unaware as they abuse the planet. It's not God's fault that there are environmental repercussions as Mother Earth is trying to rebalance herself.

ROSE

Rose suffered a horrific childhood of physical and emotional abuse. Unfortunately, at fifty-five she is still suffering. She not only blames her parents, but she blames God so strongly that she believes that anyone who speaks of "God" is not allowed in her presence. When her youngest daughter, Lyn, and fiancé Robin were planning their wedding they asked me to be their wedding officiate. Robin was raised

Christian. It was important to him that I incorporate the name "God" into the ceremony. When Rose learned this from a discussion with her daughter, she flashed into anger and began yelling that it was unacceptable to use the word "God" in their ceremony. Lyn and Robin called me to discuss the situation and asked me to mediate between them and Rose.

Parents of a wedding couple can become controlling and overlook whose wedding it really is. I called Rose, trying to calm and reassure her that Lyn and Robin didn't want to insult her belief systems, nor did they want to insult Robin's family. I asked her about her and her groom's wedding and their choices. She shared fond memories of her special day. I then asked her if she would allow her daughter, and soon to be son-in-law, to have their special day just as they dream it to be.

After she vented her fears and feelings she finally agreed to back off and honor Lyn and Robin's desires. The bride and groom agreed that they would be happy with just one mention of God, for the benefit of his family. They wanted their ceremony to be mostly non-denominational. The day went perfectly and both families were happy.

Rose has remained stuck in anger and resentment toward God and her family. This disconnect has caused her years of anxiety and temper tantrums. And needless to say, has affected all her relationships.

Pay attention to your fears and your beliefs. Shed false information and your perception that the Universe is not on your side. Take a deep breath, hold it for a couple of seconds as you think about your current fear, then exhale completely with the intention of fully releasing that fear from your mind. Repeat this positive, affirmative thought strongly and loudly:

> *Thank you, God, for taking this fear from me. I surrender it to You. I fully accept the wholeness You bring to and through me. With every breath I take, I then release, and I let go. I feel your love, and I am grateful. Blessed Be.*

I recommend that you practice this exercise, along with the STOP light, whenever a fear surfaces. What you are doing is releasing the mind's lies and replacing them with the Soul's Truth.

When a shift needs to take place, you are the only one that can make that happen in your awareness and in your life. Old beliefs that bring anger and resentment need to be released and replaced. This will allow you to become more fully conscious and aware, allowing you to feel your connection to the Source, knowing there is NO-thing to fear.

The Pathway to God

There is no right or wrong pathway to God. In interfaith studies, there is rich, fulfilling information on all the world's traditions. It does not matter how we get there, the names we use, or the stories we tell. The point is to get on the path to your Source and walk the talk.

We know people have been killed in the name of one god or another. However, my God knows nothing of killing. Fear kills. Humans kill. Egos kill. Thoughts can kill our body. Words can kill our relationships. Pay attention to your thoughts. Are you thinking thoughts filled with criticism, judgment, hate, anger, bigotry, blame, or revenge? If we want to walk the God-like path, our thoughts must be God-like. Does that mean we must be perfect? No. God does not expect us to be perfect. God expects us to be human beings moving toward awareness, mindfulness, consciousness, and enlightenment.

I have been on my path of spiritual discovery for many decades. I see no end to the path. It is now my lifestyle. I am happier and more content on this path than on any other path I have ever walked. I have chosen a spiritual path, because the path of ignorance and fear failed me. Thoughts of kindness and compassion, along with awareness, forgiveness, gratitude, and love, are the gifts of the Divine that I embrace.

Trusting the Promise

Every valley shall be lifted and filled up, and every mountain and hill shall be made low; and the crooked and uneven shall be made straight and level, and the rough places a plain.

—Isaiah 40:4

God promised us that all our crooked paths would be made straight. I know the Truth of this in my life. There have been numerous times in this journey when I have had no idea how, when, where, or why Source has called me to learn, grow, and serve in a certain way. When this happens, I immediately go into prayer. Here's an example of how I pray:

All right, God (I hear myself saying), *I hear you calling me. I don't know how to do what you're asking me to do. It's bigger than I am. I don't know how I will be able to put in all the necessary work, but I know you have all the answers. You are moving the mountains and straightening the path for me. I completely surrender the details to you. I will keep my promise, say "yes," show up, do what is required of me, and live on purpose. I turn everything over to you. Help me, God, and show me the way. Thank you, God, for bringing this opportunity to me. I trust I will experience it with ease and grace. I am filled with Divine love, and I am blessed! Amen.*

Say your own prayer, then let it go. Don't keep chewing on it. Don't let ego take you into doubt again. Stay focused and practice trust.

Spiritual Disconnection

From the day we are born, we are on the quest to return to the energy of the Supreme Source, the Beloved, to God, to the Source of ALL THAT IS. This is because we have forgotten that the Source is within us. Somewhere along the way, we became disconnected. This disconnect may have come through our family's disbelief or in anger at God and/or the teachings of separatism that show up in many religious beliefs.

The collective consciousness of negativity challenges us to stay connected spiritually. Ego doesn't want us to be connected to the One energy and will continually try to pull us out of it.

It is interesting that many people I have met who were raised with strong religious traditions often leave those traditions to go in search of something else. As I have explored numerous paths and traditions, I see they all eventually come together. All paths lead to love. What joy it is when I see that all these paths lead home to the same God. It has been right here all along…right here within us.

Misalignment

Dion Fortune wrote, "*No one particular route can be laid down as the true path or system by which every man must come. The ways to God are as many as the breaths of the sons of men. It is the directness or indirectness of the route that counts.*"

She also wrote that "*…some people might alter their path*" and cautions the would-be-student not to obey a teacher who is clearly doing wrong. "*The student has the right to judge what is or is not morally right, and should bear that in mind in times of question.*" Fortune insists that "*Thou shalt love the Lord thy God with all thy heart, and with all* *thy soul, and with all thy strength,"* and *"Him only shalt thou serve."* The function of the teacher, Initiator, fraternity, or order, *"is to bring you to God, not to take the place of God and demand your loyalty."* [35]

EUGENA

This client, who came to me several years ago requesting spiritual counseling, felt disconnected not only from her self, but from her Source. As I was collecting information from her regarding her personal growth journey, Eugena shared that she had been studying with a "teacher" for the last few years and was realizing that she felt more lost and fearful than when she had begun her studies. Eugena added that she felt manipulated and controlled by this person. Her teacher told her to never study with anyone else, to avoid all other classes, and to only seek advice and instruction from her personally.

All the red flags were waving, but Eugena, in her craving for Divine connection and guidance, not only walked past the red flags, but invested all her savings in the teacher and her trainings, only to later feel used and betrayed.

Today, Eugena has released and let go of all physical, emotional, mental, and energetic connections to that teacher. She has moved into her personal empowerment and her own voice. In our work together, she encountered many wounds that needed healing and many fears to be released.

---

35   Dion Fortune, *Esoteric Orders and Their Work* (New York: Samuel Weiser, Inc., 2000), pp. 105, 100.

She has learned discernment as she chooses trainings and classes to enrich her personal growth and assist her in how she serves in the world.

Pay attention to your intuition when choosing your personal coach, counselor, or teacher. If anything feels negative, walk away and seek guidance only from those you trust and feel is Divinely connected to their creator.

Staying Connected to Source

If we are unaware of spiritual guidance, we are unable to draw upon it. Our Source does not leave us. We leave it.

Staying connected to the Divine Intelligence of Source takes commitment. *"Practicing the presence of God"*[36] is a phrase used in many faiths. These words sum up how we may choose to live. Whatever we want to get better at, we must practice it regularly. The presence of the Divine energy of our Holy One is so wonderful that once we experience it, we want more. So how do we get more?

It's our individual choice. I enjoy my spiritual community and attending events with like-minded people. I enjoy studying spiritual works. I attend gatherings where other spiritual people bring God's messages forward.

> *For where two or three are gathered together in my name, there am I in the midst of them.*
> —Matthew 18:20

---

36   Brother Lawrence, *The Practice of the Presence of God and the Spiritual Maxims* (New York: Benton Publishing Group, 2013).

In my home, I enjoy statues and images of the Buddha, Kwan Yin, Lakshmi, Lord Ganesh, the so-called Venus of Willendorf, images of Mother Mary and Baby Jesus, and the Maitreya Buddha. I have chosen to create an environment that allows me to continually access and dwell in the presence of God's energy while at the same time I know this energy is within me. Therefore, there is no place in the world for me where God is not present.

Affirmational Prayer

Mother, Father, God, Goddess, I chose to connect to, and maintain a connection to, the Divine energy of this Universe. I ask for Your support in helping me to always feel your presence within me and around me.

I chose to practice the presence. I choose to walk my path of connection to my authentic self. I choose to live in this moment, where You reside. I choose to model my behavior and thoughts after the Master Teachers that are, and were, demonstrations of the Divine right here on earth.

I feel deep gratitude for discoveries of my Soul's purpose, my Soul's longing, my Soul's Oneness and greatness. I feel loved and I easily share love. I claim my inner Light Being. I love myself. I listen to Your guidance. I rest in the comfort of knowing I am safe, I am provided with all I need, and You have my back.

I receive my good with a grateful heart.
Amen!

WHAT IS DEATH?

Fear of Death

Being human is a strange and funny experience. It's all about staying in the awareness of love while we experience beginnings, endings, death, and transformation. Our life's phases represent small deaths that are all endings for something.

Death is the ultimate "disconnect"...or is it? Humans believe in death. But God does not. God doesn't die and neither do we. We live on forever, just in a different form. As human beings, we become attached to our physical bodies and the physical bodies of our loved ones.

There are many beliefs as to whether there is life after death. The question is whether life after death would be close to what we experience here and now. I think it's doubtful. Because we would no longer have the experience of the physical body, our experience would be different. Remembering that we are not this body, but are IN this body, therefore, would we not have an out of body experience

(OOBE)[37] when we transition? Do we find peace within the body, or do we find peace when we allow ourselves to enter a different awareness or another dimension? Consider these issues and journal accordingly.

Grief

If you come to visit my grave, my tomb will appear to dance!

—Rumi[38]

I took hospice volunteer training to serve those who are actively dying and their grieving families. Hospice training teaches that Dr. Elizabeth Kübler-Ross[39], a leader and author in the death and dying arena, described the five stages of grief: denial or shock, then bargaining; then anger, resentment, even rage; then despair or depression; and finally acceptance and recovery.

Grieving is non-linear, however, and we may go in and out of each of these stages throughout the grieving process.

---

37 Defined by the Paranormal Encyclopedia.com as the sensation of one's consciousness or spirit separating from one's physical body. About 95% of the world's cultures include a belief in the out of body experience.

38 Jalāl ad-Dīn Muhammad Rūmī, known in the English-speaking world as Rumi, was a 13th-century Persian poet, jurist, theologian, and Sufi mystic.

39 Elisabeth Kübler-Ross, M.D., was a Swiss-born psychiatrist, humanitarian, co-founder of the hospice movement around the world, and the author of *On Death and Dying* (1969), which first presented the five stages of grief.

Denial, or shock, is a normal experience when we are in the disbelief stage of our loss. Bargaining is when we may say to God, "Take me. Let my child live," or "I will stop smoking if you just take this cancer away." We may feel anger, resentment, and outrage at God, the Universe, our family, or others, as we blame that which took away the one we love or the things we had. We experience depression or despair, angst, suffering, feeling hopeless, helpless, loss, and emptiness.

At the point of recovery, we move into acceptance and the ability to live with our loss. We then can move on with our life, still having memories of the past but allowing a letting-go process to take place in a healthy way.

If a person avoids or delays the grieving process, that empty, angry, depressive energy continues and can create mental, emotional, spiritual, and possibly physical disease.

Transformation Itself

As I was writing this book, my beloved brother, Ken, transitioned from the physical plane to the spiritual plane. I wrote the following shortly before his passing. I share it with you now in its original state.

As I experience yet another beautiful seasonal change here in the Rocky Mountains, I breathe the crisp fall air and marvel at the vibrant colors the leaves are demonstrating. With everyone's expectation, Mother Earth's transformation is filled with grace and beauty. This, along with spring, is my favorite time of year. I feel more alive during the essence of rebirth and death. Transformation itself.

At this very moment, my youngest brother is experiencing a major transformation. The brain cancer abruptly took Ken from the late summer of his life into fall as his body became weaker and weaker from the many forms of toxic treatment he received.

During the last fifteen months of his physical challenge, he has lost a great deal of vitality, but not hope. His body is heading into its hibernation, its time of dormancy. They say the brain cancer that originally brought him to his knees has now entered his brain stem, and the long months of invasive treatments and hospital stays have drained the life force from his body and his mind. The infection (MRSA[40]) that has taken over and can no longer be controlled, appears to be winning.

As I see the beautiful leaves fall from the trees, now lifeless, no longer filled with the green of health and strength, I think of my brother. Beautiful, but withering, a vibrant Soul, yet dying. I know the Truth that this is only an illusion. To sustain

---

40 *Methicillin-resistant Staphylococcus Aureus* (MRSA) is an infection caused by a strain of staph bacteria that have become resistant to the antibiotics commonly used to treat ordinary staph infections. (see www.mayoclinic.com)

me during this sad time, I look at the evergreens that cover our mountains and hold their vitality through all seasons, year after year. I also remember this is the Truth of our Soul.

In the Hindu holy book, the Bhagavad-Gita, Lord Krishna[41] responds to Arjuna's concern about leading the righteous Pandava clan into battle against their kin, the evil sons of Dhritarashtra: "The truly wise mourn neither for the living nor for the dead," says Lord Krishna. "Just as the dweller in this body passes through childhood, youth, and old age, so at death he merely passes into another kind of body. Bodies are said to die, but That which possesses the body is eternal. It cannot be limited, or destroyed. Death is certain for the born. Rebirth is certain for the dead. You should not grieve for what is unavoidable."

As I enjoy and rejoice at the changing of the seasons, and the magnificence of fall, I know winter will come. It, too, has its own beauty. As with my brother's journey of transformation, he, too, will soon move into the next stage of his time, his next season, and his next experience. I remember the Truth that at the core of Ken is

---

41 Lord Krishna is the Divine incarnate and the essence of the *Bhagavad-Gita Gait*, the Hindu scripture. See Narasimha Ramayya Nathamuni, *Lord Krishna: The Lord of the Universe, Vol. 1 & 2* (Hyderabad, India: Sridhar Nadamvni, 2011).

his Soul. The Soul never dies, It continues forever, and just as the green on the trees will reappear in the spring, our Soul continually experiences rebirth through Its next path. And so It goes, and so It is!

Nirvana is "Life's goal," according to the Buddha, who used fire as an example: "to blow out" or "to extinguish." Nirvana, it is said, is the highest destiny of the human spirit; it is boundless life Itself. When our fire (physical life) is extinguished, all we need to know is that the condition is beyond the limitations of mind, thoughts, feelings, and will. The Buddha says, "Bliss, yes, bliss, my friends, is Nirvana."

These concepts have never been stronger for me than now. I experienced my brother's transition, gently holding his hand in mine on that day in October 2009. At this time in my life, I have been brought to the greatest level of reflection, wonder, and even discomfort, as I have pondered the experience of my brother's journey. I did not expect him to feel so far away from me when he left his body. I expected to still feel his Soul nearby, and I believe one day I will again, even though at this time as he feels to me so detached from this earth-plane. I witness with remorse, how attached to the Earth I still feel.

Our Spiritual Body

Fear is a lack of connection to knowing yourself as Spirit in form. Spirit never dies. We never die. The body is a temporary vehicle. You are in your body, but you are not your body. This temporary vessel is a package for the Soul.

I have often thought about the fact that without the body I would not have to work. We work to support the feeding and caring of the body, don't we? We have to house it, feed it, transport it, clothe it, decorate it, and eventually bury it in some celebratory way. Yet while we are in it, it brings us both great pleasure and great pain.

As a volunteer at an elders' memory care facility and now in the hospice community, I have lost many friends because transition is a weekly event. It is humbling to witness so many departures. Their faces, smiles, love, and sometimes evidence of decline and death stay with me.

Where Is Heaven? Where Is Hell?

After the death of my brother, who was my grand niece's grandfather and from whom she was estranged, my grand niece asked me one evening as we sipped our tea, "Do you think Ken is going to hell?"

Her question surprised me, and I asked her, "Why would you think he is going to hell?"

"Well," she said, "has he taken Jesus Christ as his Lord and Savior?"

"No, probably not," I answered. "However, in my

understanding of God, God does not judge. People do. God, through Jesus, did not teach judgment. Jesus taught unconditional love and acceptance of all, from the lepers he healed, to the disbelievers and so called sinners, to his followers, his disciples, and the believers. All are equally loved."

Heaven and hell are not destination points. I believe both are right here on earth. As we believe, so shall we create. We will experience the essence of heaven or hell based on where we think we are. Heaven is here in this moment. It's not a place outside one's self. The perception that you are having a "hellish" experience will create that "hellish" experience in your awareness.

The Universe always answers us with a loud yes to whatever belief we stand in. Just think about the power you carry in every one of your thoughts. With this power, however, there is great responsibility to yourself and your world. Do you misuse it by focusing on the illusions of past hurts and challenges? Do not cling to your past with regret. Live in the present moment with love.

Everyone has the opportunity and the choice to either be a victim or to rise above the situation and move into trust and love. This does not mean we stuff our emotions or pretend all is well. What it means is that we witness the circumstances we have drawn into our lives. We pay attention and learn the lesson that was brought forth. We have the power of choice. We have the power to set healthy boundaries and to love and take care of ourselves as we heal from a challenge. We have the choice to move out of fear, anger, blaming, and revenge and into forgiveness—first to forgive ourselves. Forgiveness and self-healing are inside jobs. Only after we've forgiven ourselves can we forgive others. Here is another opportunity to process and journal what comes up for you.

The Journey

So where do we go when we die? People wonder, pontificate, guess, predict, and try to control the answer to this question. My belief is that when we shed this vessel called our body, our Soul is free to BE aware of Its Oneness with the One Great Soul. I chose to believe that I will reunite with my loved ones who have passed before me. I chose to believe that I will experience a witnessing of what I created, or destroyed, while in my human form. What did I leave behind? Did I leave a legacy of love or one of pain?

We all have choices, right now, to create that which we will revisit later on the next step of our Soul's journey. What we do in every moment has a rippling effect throughout time. Now is the only NOW you have in which to learn, grow, heal, forgive, repair, release, and create that, by which you want to be remembered. I recently heard someone say that "some day" is not a day of the week. Some day does not exist. We only have this moment. I believe that the *only* thing that remains is love.

I am not here to change your mind or make you believe what I believe. We all have a right to our own opinions.

FREDERICK

I recently had a deep conversation with a brilliant and wise fifteen-year-old boy named Frederick, who shared what he wants his legacy to be when he leaves this incarnation. He said he wants to be remembered as a good person, as a loving, and kind person. He wants his future children to think kindly of their father, to remember him with deep love and respect as a role model. He hopes they will want to be just like him. He also said he wants to make a difference in the world and in his career of choice. After he passes, Frederick wants people to speak well of him.

I share this story here because of how significant this dream is for this young man at this time in his life. Frederick is in crisis. He is having a personal struggle with finding the loving part of himself. He has been struggling with his self-worth, his self-esteem, who he is, and why he was verbally abused as a child. At this time, he is in great pain and is feeling angst and fear. He is struggling. Teenagers often go through deep introspective challenges. It can be a scary, overwhelming time for them. I am honored to work with this Soul in his teenage body, to assist him to heal and become the kind man he dreams of being.

How do you want to be remembered? What legacy do you want to leave to your family? To this planet? What can you repair before you go? What can you forgive now?

I believe that when we finish what we've come here to do, no matter how young or old we are, that's when we leave this place. Not before. No one else, no thing else, makes that decision for us, no matter how it appears. It is completely our Soul's choice. That said, of course, we never really know when we've finished what we came here to do

Lillian, My Mother

As my son lowered his grandmother's ashes into a small grave near the headstone of his great grandmother's grave, I could not watch. It was too painful. We had chosen to place the remains of mother and daughter together, knowing they would love that. I was officiating my mother's graveside memorial service. This was one of the most difficult tasks I have ever had to carry out. My tears choked my words.

We had a memorial table nearby. It was covered with framed pictures of my mother living her life. I took the large vase holding a variety of flowers that included her favorite yellow roses from the table and busied myself distributing the flowers to the family mourners. We would be placing them on her grave. All the while, a beautiful rendition of "The Old Rugged Cross" was playing in the background. For as long as I can remember, my mother asked for this song to be played at her funeral, just as it had been played at her mother's funeral.

After prayers and the eulogy had been delivered, my family shared their favorite memories of Lillian. Then my son helped me place the first shovel of dirt in the small hole that now held the container of my mother's remains. My knees weakened.

In my heart, I believe my brother and grandmother

greeted my mother's Soul when she left her body. During the service, several family members saw two different yellow birds, one in a tree and one on a telephone wire, watching the memorial for about thirty minutes. I could feel the energy of my mother and my grandmother during the service. I believe those birds were the forms my mother and grandmother took to show themselves to us.

The day my mother died and for two days after, I could not breathe. My grief was so heavy, it weighed upon my chest and throat. My sobs were deep, the tears would not stop. When I walked, I could not feel my feet on the floor.

I did not understand my experience because I had already been grieving the loss of my mother for many years. First dementia, then Alzheimer's disease took the mother I knew. After my brother passed in 2009, my mother's health declined exponentially. After years of grieving her pending death, I didn't expect her actual death to be such a shock to my system.

The heaviness finally lifted, but the grieving still has not.

Relying on my support system gave me the opportunity to begin to feel grounded again. I am sensitive to the awareness that groundedness feels different now, but there is healing in my understanding. I am also aware of the many layers of past life and karmic energies that have cleared for me in this transformative time. My mother transitioned and transformed. As have I.

After speaking with a dear friend, I have come to a spiritual realization that it is our mother who keeps us tethered to the Earth-plane until she leaves it. A mother could have abandoned us a hundred different ways during our lifetime, and abandonment is always painful. But it is not as painful as when the existential cord to this earthly plane is pulled. Our mother brought us into this life experience and she metaphorically keeps us grounded here. It now makes sense to me why I could not feel my feet touch the floor after my mother left this dimension. I am now on my own. I have to find my own footing. I not only grieve the loss of my mother's physical presence, but I also miss what she provided to me as a "earthly" anchor.

When I sat with my brother on the day of his death, I felt his feet become cold to my touch. When I commented on this to a nurse standing nearby, she replied that as we are leaving this earth, we disconnect first through our feet. Ken was gone only a few minutes later.

As I have meditated on what the nurse said, I have gained an understanding of the dramatic and traumatic experience we all seem to have with the loss of our mothers. Clients and friends have told me how the loss of their mother was their worst experience. I have lost many loved ones in my life, but the loss of my mother has been the most difficult.

Processing Time

Death and grief are heavy topics and may trigger your own grief. Take your journal out now and process anything that comes up for you. Some questions to ponder are:

- Am I currently in a grieving process?
- What stage of grief, do I feel I am in right now?
- Do I have a support system as I grieve?
- What do I need to grieve?
- Do I understand grief?
- Do I fear feeling grief?
- Am I avoiding grief?

Take as much time as you need. Allow yourself to really feel your feelings. With all the layers of grieving that are necessary for your healing, you will experience many growth opportunities. Be grateful for what this challenge brings you to heal.

LORI ANN

In April 1964, I gave birth to a seven-pound baby girl and I named her Lori Ann. In those days, a newborn baby was not instantly placed in the mother's arms. My baby was taken away to be cleaned up and I didn't think anything of Lori Ann's absence. I was taken to a ward of five other new mothers, where I waited for Lori Ann to be brought to me. Hours passed.

When I saw all the other babies brought in to be fed by their mothers, and mine was not brought to me, I asked the nurse for my baby. She said I would have to talk to my doctor. This immediately brought fear into my heart.

The doctor finally came and told me that Lori Ann had been born with a deformed heart. When she was a three-month-old fetus, the left side of her heart had stopped developing, but because she was living through my blood supply, her situation had not been detected. In 1964, CAT scans and ultrasounds were nonexistent. My doctor was not aware of the life-threatening condition of my daughter until she was born.

They put Lori Ann in an incubator. When I asked to see her, they told me I had to stay in bed. I was only nineteen years old then, and I didn't have the voice I have today. It was when my husband insisted I be allowed to see Lori Ann that I was finally wheeled to the nursery so I could look at her through the glass window. She was lying on her right side, facing me. They would not allow me into the nursery, and they would not allow me to hold her. My only memory of my child, beyond carrying her for nine months and giving birth, was seeing her little moon-shaped face looking back at me through the window. She looked so alone.

The day of her birth, the doctor told me that the next day my baby would go into surgery for a heart catheterization to better determine her condition. When I asked him about her chances of survival, he said it was minimal. Lori Ann died during the procedure. She was only two days old. She never felt the touch of her mother. I never held my child.

The treatment of patients in the 1960s was often antiquated and cruel. When the nurses brought medication, I didn't know that they were giving me antidepressant/anxiety medication. Back then, women usually spent a full week in the hospital after giving birth, so I thought nothing of it when they told me I couldn't leave. I had no advocate. Neither my husband nor my mother spotted anything wrong with the hospital's treatment of me. No one questioned the doctors or nurses, who would not deal with me when I told them I wanted to leave. The nurses and doctors did not want me to feel or be emotional, so they gave me what I came to call "happy pills."

I was not allowed to leave the hospital to go to my daughter's funeral. My mother and husband handled all the arrangements. I was young, immature, in shock, and unaware of what was happening. I believed I had no rights. Unfortunately, this is what could happen when people gave their power and trust to medical and hospital staff.

I was released from the hospital at the end of the week, after my daughter's burial. I went home to my eleven-month-old son, without grief counseling or any guidance whatsoever. I was confused, numb, shocked, and emotionally alone. No one wanted to talk about what I had gone through. My first husband was verbally abusive and non-supportive, physically and emotionally. Within a few months after Lori Ann's passing, I took my son and ran home to my mother.

At age nineteen, I knew nothing about the grieving process. I was very depressed and nonfunctional. Please remember, there is no "official" timeframe within which to grieve. Grief gives us a life-long opportunity to heal, release, feel, cry, and heal some more. It is done in layers. Yes, there are five steps in grieving, but by no means is grieving a linear path. Again, being kind to yourself is extremely important. Eventually I learned about the grieving process and moved forward. I grieved for many years, the best way I knew how.

Grief Revisited

Thirty years later, I was alone one evening, watching a television documentary about two families who had newborn babies with health challenges. One family living on the east coast had a baby that had been born with a major brain challenge. It had died soon after birth. The family on the west coast had a baby with a defective heart. It needed a transplant. The documentary was about harvesting the east coast infant's heart and transporting it across country to be transplanted into the waiting west coast baby's body.

All of a sudden and without warning, my emotions took over and a guttural cry came up from the depth of my Soul. I did not try to stop it. I had an out-of-body experience during which I could see and hear myself as this deeper level of grief was surfacing. I felt the energy of God around me, supporting me. Almost immediately, I was given the reason behind the new level of grief I was experiencing. I was grieving because when my baby girl needed a heart transplant, the technique was not yet available. I was grieving that my Lori Ann never had any hope of survival.

This major awareness was brought to me not only for my healing, but also so I could share it with others. And for this, I am grateful.

Karma

Those who believe in past lives and reincarnation usually believe in karma. But there can be misunderstandings of karmic energy. Karma means action of cause and effect. Experiencing karma is for growth and learning, never for punishment. God gave our Soul a choice to reincarnate or not. Reincarnation is free will. Our Soul chose to reincarnate into the physical experience again for the purpose of having another opportunity to work on the issues we have not yet completed. Our journey here is to gain full awareness of the Soul, and the best way to do that is through our spiritual practice.

Karma gives us the opportunity to learn and learn again until we "get it," whatever "it" is. When we continually repeat certain situations and attract certain types of people into our lives, we may be working through karma.

It's a good idea to take responsibility for your own karma. How you react in relationship to others creates your karma. Karma may bring us together. Every major connection to another individual is chosen by our Soul for the opportunity to grow and learn. We are each other's teachers.

"Oh, my dear, karma is only a bitch if you are."
—Unknown

Karma is an individual matter. It keeps moving us along our path to God. All of our searches in life are ultimately for the purpose of finding our way to our original Source. When we figure out why we behave the way we do, why we have tendencies to behave in ways that create negativity in our lives, and when we choose to stop the behavior, we can finally break the karmic hold. Everyone is responsible for his or her own karma. How do you behave? Do you treat others with disrespect, sarcasm, and abusive language? Look at your habits. Do they bring the results you desire or the benefits you would like into your life? Both your thoughts and your actions create your karma. Condemning others through our thoughts is as destructive as physically attacking them.

Take a serious look at your behavior, your thought patterns, habits, and actions. What are they? Write about them in your journal. This is another opportunity to reflect on where you are and where you want to be. Make a decision to eliminate negative behavior. Refuse to allow your egoic mind to keep you in darkness and karmic repetition. Focus on creating new habits that will nurture you. Work to lift your consciousness. Allow yourself to be led to the Divine. When we make God our focus, we elevate ourselves. Then we burn off karma.

There may be times in our life when we feel we must have done something right because we are experiencing "good" karma. Not so. There really are not good or bad karma. It's cause and effect. We are always blessed and we are always learning, no matter what appears to be happening.

Angels

I am not an expert on angels, but I have been blessed with many in my life. There are the big archangels and the little angels that work and walk with me on my spiritual and metaphysical paths. In addition, there are angels that have shown up in my life in the form of physical beings. One particular Soul comes to mind—someone who influenced my life completely. He was truly my angel. I must admit, however, that at the time I did not understand how my relationship with my stepfather would mold me into who I am today. Twenty years ago, I had a revelation. I love revelations. Not only my own, but witnessing others discovering theirs.

My Revelation

When I was ten years old, my mother remarried. Her new husband, Jack, was kind to me and taught me many life values. He was the first person that I ever felt really saw and heard me. He actually talked with me. He was more of a father to me than my abusive biological father ever was. I called him Dad. When I was eighteen, my mother and stepfather divorced. At that time in my life, I was enmeshed with my mother, so I took her side and never spoke to Jack again. I stopped calling him Dad.

It was not until I was well into my forties that I had a deep revelation of how much love and respect I had for Jack. But when I realized this, I learned he had already died. So there I was, thirty-some years later, grieving my loss of him for the first time. I finally realized just how much he had influenced my entire life. In my heart, I began calling him Dad again because he had truly played that role for me. I will always be grateful to him.

We were together for eight years during the most formative teenage period of my life, from middle school through high school. When I was eleven years old, my dad suggested and set up the opportunity for me to be in a marching band as a little majorette. My mother didn't like to be bothered with these things, but Dad drove me to practice every week and then all over the state to march and perform.

Dad taught me how to swim. He taught us the importance of being involved in the community. My fondest memories are all the times he was there for me. He was the one who helped me with my homework. He taught me how to do research so I could write the best papers I possibly could. He was with me when I practiced my speeches for English class and taught me how to deliver a quality presentation. We stayed up late together many nights perfecting my skills. Dad celebrated my gold stars.

He was my champion. He stuck up for me when my seventh-grade geography teacher gave me an F because she said the American Indian art project I turned in was too good for my age. Dad immediately went to the principal's office with me, and we met with that teacher and the principal. He told them how he had offered to help me on that project and how I had refused because I wanted to do it all myself. They raised the grade to a D. But my Dad told me he knew it should have been an A and he was proud of me. He was the one who introduced me to opera, classical music, ballet, and the arts. And when I was in high school, Dad was the one who attended my school performances.

Looking back, my mother seemed to only be a dim glimmer in the background. She was not interested in, or supportive of, me. I thank God for giving me an angel-Dad.

During my grieving, all those years later, I wrote him many letters filled with gratitude and love. I know that because of his support, training, and encouragement, I am who I am today. I am the researcher, the writer/author, the speaker/presenter, the creator, teacher, the business owner, and the life-long student. He would be very proud of me. I believe he was at my ordination, standing there and applauding. I miss him, respect him, and love him still.

I am so grateful for this revelation. I might have lived the rest of my life oblivious to the tremendous gift that God brought me…my true father.

Please move into reflection. In your journal name the person or the people who are or have been angels in your life. What did they bring to you? Have you been an angel to someone else? How? Do you want to be an angel? Explore and seek guidance on your path of self-discovery! You deserve it.

A Guided Meditation #6

(You may want to record this meditation.)

Allow yourself to become comfortable where you sit. Noticing where your body touches the chair, the pillow, or the floor, take a deep, cleansing breath. Releasing all extraneous thoughts, focus only on your breathing.

Your level of awareness naturally deepens now, as you count very slowly, backward from 10...9, 8, 7, 6, 5, 4, 3, 2, and 1. Taking this opportunity for yourself to move into and receive healing, you begin to feel the warmth of golden light surrounding you. Continue to breathe deeply.

Now become aware that you are barefoot. You're walking on cool, green grass. All around you are many trees, and you smell the fresh, clean air of the mountains. You notice that to one side there are picnic tables, but no people are around. It is peaceful here. You hear the movement of water. Your attention is pulled to just beyond the flowering lilac bushes to a rushing, bubbling creek. This creek is fed by the snow melting on the surrounding mountains. The water is playing over the rocks that are scattered through the creek bottom. The sound is melodic and centers you deeply into your Soul. You walk beside the creek, following the water on its journey east.

Soon you are led to sit on a large boulder overlooking the creek at a juncture where there are many rocks blocking the flow of the crystal clear mountain water. You notice the flow of water has been diminished to a slow, steady trickle. The water cannot flow freely here.

As you close your eyes to move deeper within your being, you clearly hear guidance giving you a message regarding the rocks (blocks) that are impeding your own flow, the flow of abundance of good in your life. Hear that message clearly now. Take your time.

After you receive your message, you are given a breathtaking vision in which you see that the largest boulders blocking the water's flow are suddenly lit with rays of bright sunlight shining down through the overhanging trees. As the sunlight dances on the water and on these huge rocks, the rocks are instantly transformed into giant rainbow crystal spheres! These crystals are radiating deep healing energy that moves vibrantly through your entire body. Allow yourself to bask in this healing energy.

When you are ready, take another deep breath. You are guided to open your eyes. You look in amazement at the creek. What you see now is a miracle—the water is flowing freely, gleefully, rushing over and through the rocks. The sunlight shining brightly on the water makes it look like diamonds and crystals. You know this is symbolic. Intuitively you know that you have released your own blocks during the powerful vision you were given. Promise yourself that you will come here again. Promise yourself that you will release all beliefs that are blocking you from receiving Good in your life.

It is time to leave this sacred space now. You climb down from the boulder and return to the grass. You walk back toward where you began this journey. Giving thanks to your guidance, the boulders, the creek, the water, and the mountains—you allow your awareness to move back to your breathing and to your physical body. Take three deep breaths and slowly open your eyes.

Welcome back. Open your journal and document

your experience on this journey. What was the message from your guidance? What blocks did you release?

Affirmational Prayer

This prayer is written for you to speak to your God. Take a deep breath. The breath of life. God's life.

As Divine Love flows through me as me, I know every breath I take is Great Spirit in form. Therefore, I cannot be anything but whole and holy, healthy and healing.

God's intention is for me to experience only good. I honor my personal connection to Spirit and draw to myself complete health, abundant prosperity, and magnificent happiness!

I release all fears, worries, and blocks into the Universal Law of Circulation, knowing that as I give my trust and faith to the Source by releasing, I receive that which I believe is my Good. I live in gratitude, thankfulness, and mindfulness as I heal and grow stronger mentally, emotionally, spiritually, and physically.

I am comforted in knowing that my loved ones' Souls continue, whether in the physical form or the spiritual form. The Soul always IS. Allowing Universal support to be with me during my times of grief sustains me. I remember I am never alone.

And as I know that God never leaves me I know that I will still be walking with God when I leave this physical plane. At that time I will remember, and return to, that from which I came.

The inner rush of grace and unconditional love from God and for God flows through me. I am reminded that ALL is in perfect order. I feel peace in my center. I feel Universal support. I feel the I AM, as I know I AM the favored one. I experience the full sense of well-being and gladness that lets me know that ALL is well. God has again touched my life in the now.

The Source of All that IS is everywhere, all the time, in every one. With this full knowing, I am deeply grateful. I am so blessed! Amen, Aho, Ashe', Blessed Be.

Final Message:

I don't know what I am doing! But God does—and I just say, "YES!" When I finish this *earth-walk* I expect to be greeted by my loved ones and my God/Goddess.

I wish you all a peaceful, joyous, wonderful, happy, loving, and abundant Soul journey to enlightenment.

See you on the other side.

Namaste and Ashe

Rev. Judy

ABOUT THE AUTHOR

The Reverend Judy Miller-Dienst is an internationally known medical intuitive and metaphysical integrative teacher and lecturer on spiritual healing, medical intuition, and the relationship between body, mind, and Soul. She is the founder and president of The Mystery School, Inc., in Boulder, Colorado, which offers trainings in a variety of metaphysical and body/mind/spirit studies. As a longtime student of New Thought, as well as the Goddess, Wiccan, Gnostic, Native American, and Interfaith traditions, Rev. Judy has an eclectic spiritual background that serves as a strong foundational support to her teachings.

As an ordained interfaith minister (and alumna of The New Seminary in New York), Rev. Judy is an associate minister for the Interfaith Temple of NYC. She is the founder of Omni-Faith Ministry, a division of The Mystery School, Inc., and serves from the Boulder Valley, Colorado, area. Performing weddings, baby blessings, memorial and funeral services, as well as delivering her powerful messages at churches and spiritual centers, bring her peace and joy.

Rev. Judy joyously brings her phenomenal abilities forward as a clairvoyant, clairsentient, clairaudient, as well as demonstrates the prophetic-knowing. She began her studies in mind science and medical intuition in 1976. She has been in private practice since 1991.

She produced and hosted the *Healing Voices* cable television show in Long Beach, California, for four years and the *Healing Voices* radio show on KGNU in Boulder, Colorado. *Healing Voices* focused on holistic and complementary healing and spiritual development. She has been a frequent media guest and is a former newspaper contributor.

Rev. Judy lives in a small, tranquil town in northern Colorado where the snowcapped Rocky Mountains touch the sky. She lives with her tabby cat, Rumi, who continues to train her to be all that he wants her to be and Spirit, her little calico girl who is the sweetest lap kitty ever. Her cherished son and grandsons live nearby. Volunteering in her community, Rev. Judy remains focused on serving.

For sacred ceremonies, guest speaking, and private sessions, please visit Rev. Judy at www.themysteryschool. org. Or contact her via email at dnahealer@aol.com.

Made in the USA
San Bernardino, CA
12 September 2018